ELOQUENT BODY

DAWN GARISCH

modjaji books

Also by Dawn Garisch

Not Another Love Story

Stoning the Tree

Babyshoes

Once, Two Islands

Trespass

Difficult Gifts

Publication © Modjaji Books 2012
Copyright © Dawn Garisch 2012

First published in 2012 by Modjaji Books PTY Ltd
P O Box 385, Athlone, 7760, South Africa
modjaji.books@gmail.com
http://modjaji.book.co.za
www.modjajibooks.co.za

ISBN 978-1-920397-39-5

Cover artwork: Katherine Glenday
Cover design: Nicola Glenday
Book design: Natascha Mostert and Life is Awesome Design Studio.
Thanks to publishers and authors who gave permission for quotes. Details in Endnotes.
Printed and bound by Mega Digital, Cape Town
Set in Palatino

For Luke and Jon

Contents

PART **THREE**
Tracking the Truth

PART **FOUR**
Heal Thyself

Introduction

My heart has been speaking;
so I have been taking notes

Geoffrey Godbert[1]

A few years ago, I found myself up all night, as though with a new-born. Every time I started dropping off, another thought arrived, demanding that I commit it to paper. I knew that if I left the ideas till morning, they were unlikely to survive. So I pushed myself upright again and again, scribbling on the closest paper at hand – a prescription pad from work. In the morning, wanting to transcribe what had arrived in the night, I could hardly read the notes. The muse's handwriting looks just like a doctor's.

The Great Healer of the Arts had prescribed a cure for what Richard Ford called the commotion in his chest and Virginia Woolf called a wave in the mind, otherwise known as the itch that can only be scratched by a fountain pen on paper.

The previous day, a call for applications for grants for non-fiction work had arrived in my inbox. It attracted my full attention. Life had thrown this across my track. A work of non-fiction would allow me to pursue the concerns of my novels – how to integrate the personal and the political, character and context, the use and abuse of power, old ways of being and new ways, the rational and irrational, desire and restraint. It would give me the space to explore the many other splits that I experience both within myself and within society, for I am a doctor and a novelist, a scientist and a dancer, a researcher and a poet. Sometimes they are suspicious and uneasy bedfellows.

My whole adult life I have been gathering material about the body, unconscious drives, illness, creative capacities, and how they intersect. This book, I realised, would be a place to set it all down, and to investigate the subjects further. In addition, I was frustrated by the limitations of what I am able to do as a doctor and excited by my discoveries as a writer. It became clear to me that if I were to act in the best interests of my patients – of people in general – this book was the way to proceed.

***

As a medical doctor and a writer, I have lived a split life for many years. Slowly, very slowly, I am changing from a doctor who writes into a writer who doctors. They are the two legs of my working life, and I am merely shifting my weight from one to the other. It feels right. I feel on track.

Over the years, this dual and parallel life has afforded me glimpses into the complexities of human behaviour in general, and also into the heart of my own condition. I am fascinated and concerned by the trends I see.

In the consulting room patients frequently come to me complaining of conditions that are self-inflicted. Many want a quick fix, rather than to attend to the aspects of their lives that are untenable. They are anxious, and unwilling to pay attention to their bodies. In running writing workshops, I have discovered how fearful people are of applying themselves to those things they yearn to do. I have had to find ways to assist myself and others with creative conflicts. In addition, I have a chronic illness which has forced me into the position of a patient.

Anxiety is a part of the human condition. It is to an extent innate – a normal stage of development – as we can see when an infant is handed from a parent to a stranger. We call this separation anxiety and, if it is managed well by the caregiver, the baby learns to feel secure. Anxiety is also a product of our time and the way we live – high density living, pollution, deadlines, worries about climate change, the economy and crime rates. We all have to develop strategies to deal with our fear so that we are not overwhelmed or even paralysed.

We think of ourselves as rational, logical creatures. Ours is an age of science. Yet our behaviour often contradicts logic. We live mythical lives in parallel with our physiological ones, yet we do not understand the stories, symptoms and symbols that are spliced into our flesh: the body as repository for legend and memory and dream; the body as stage or as battleground for feuding narratives; the body as foreign country to be invaded, conquered and subdued, or approached with curiosity and respect; the body as a guide and friend, assisting us, or as an enemy which obstructs our plans and dreams.

We think of the enemy as 'out there', but we often act in ways that are not in our own best interests. We are strangers to ourselves, shielded from our true natures, our desires and abilities, by self-deception, denigration and the fabrications of our time.

***

Eloquent Body is a place where the two streams of my life converge. They have been heading for this point in place and time for years; for years I have been preparing to write this manuscript without my knowing it. The book is a contribution to the pool of ideas and works that aims to find out who we are, and why we are here. It examines the drive towards life as it manifests in the body, in illness and in the creative act. It looks at how we can determine what we can trust and suggests ways of developing a partnership with ourselves, which axiomatically includes not abusing the very ground that we live off and stand on. –

I imagine there was a time when everyone around the fire was encouraged to participate in imaginative and creative acts – to dance, sing, tell stories, make music, or draw in the sand. I imagine a time when people took note of their physical and political selves as an essential part of their survival. We have become spectators, rather than participants. We watch TV, film and sport, most of the time not even leaving our homes to do so. We think only professionals know enough and are good enough to do or to make. We are even observers when it comes to politics, no longer involving ourselves in civic life, and leaving meaningful decisions and protest up to those we vote for or employ.

The body, health and creativity appear to have been abdicated by individuals and co-opted by professionals and commerce. This book investigates why we have allowed this to happen, and how it is detrimental, not only to human beings, but also to the earth. It will look at the strengths and weaknesses of the decision-making tools available to us.

The first section gives a personal account of how both my own illness and my son's accident forced me to reconsider, fundamentally, my understanding of myself, my body and how the world works. From the perspective of a medical practitioner and an artist, I contrast the different rational and non-rational strategies we employ to manage our lives. In illustrating the endemic attitudes of disregard and abuse we have towards the physical homes of our bodies and of the earth, I emphasise how essential it is to pay both consequential and non-rational attention to the distress flares of illness and injury.

The second section looks at the roles fear, anxiety and self-deception play in impeding our best efforts as I have encountered them in the consulting room and in the studio, with the body as a central motif. I illustrate how those with vested interests encourage our disconnection and fear in order to sell us a product or a way of living in both the economic and political spheres of life. I set down what psychological theory and neuroscience have to say about fear, and illustrate how our anxiety management plans often tend to make things worse. It seems that we sometimes trust where we should not, and do not trust where we should.

The third contrasts the methods scientists and artists use to investigate the truth, and looks at how these approaches can help us. It also looks at why these approaches are seemingly incompatible and often give very different answers.

In the fourth section, I suggest that we need to develop better strategies to deal with anxiety – ones that lead to better care both for ourselves and the planet. I will present a way forward, derived from the modern confluence of neuroscience, psychology and art.

***

I was born into a family and a culture where it was deemed essential to know where one was heading. I belong to a healing profession where the training harnesses knowledge and skills in the service of diagnosis and cure. These are worthy goals, yet I have come to appreciate another way of living – that of process. As a writer, I have learnt that the journey will provide information that will influence the destination. As a doctor, I have witnessed both the invaluable strengths and the shortcomings of medicine as it is currently practised, also how non-rational interventions can provide relief in surprising ways. As a patient I have come to understand that the body has an intelligence that is not accessible at present through science.

Reading this text will not be like boarding a train, settling down as the stations tickertape by in a predictable sequence, and then disembarking at a prearranged destination. There are aspects of science and art that have fascinated and assisted me, and I have some strongly held ideas that I intend to put down, but I will leave the door open for related material to interrupt what I know, and to intervene and upset where I think I am going.

The writer and explorer, W. H. Murray, had this to say:

> Concerning all acts of initiative (and creation)
> there is one elementary truth, the ignorance of
> which kills countless ideas and splendid plans:

that the moment one definitely commits oneself,
then providence moves too.[2]

The day after I received the invitation to apply for a grant,
I began to write the proposal. In the far distance I heard a
rumble. It could have been warning of an avalanche, a rapid
sequence of crushing failures – my best intentions laid waste,
but I suspected it was a stampede of angels, hurrying to assist
me.

***

PART
ONE

Talking to Myself
Across the Table

1. The Science and the Poetry of the Body

The Paradox of Life:
A bit beyond perception's reach
I sometimes believe I see
that Life is two locked boxes, each
containing the other's key.

Piet Hein[3]

The World Health Organisation's definition of health, which has not been amended since 1948, is 'a state of complete physical, mental and social well-being and not merely the absence of disease or infirmity'. This is a goal and, as with many goals, it is formulated from good intentions, but is inadequate, even misguided. Life is not a fixed state, but a dynamic process which is taking place on numerous fronts simultaneously.

How do we know whether we are 'in tune' with ourselves? How do we know what our bodies and our lives want of us? The 'sick' part of ourselves might be the healthy part which is trying to get us to change the way we live. We frequently behave as though our lives, like our bodies, are there for us to do with what we please, like vehicles we drive around in until they are ready for the scrap heap. Instead, we could regard ourselves as caretakers and co-authors of the story of our lives.

Over and above the advice of our health consultants, there is a part of us that knows what is good or right for our wellbeing and our passage. This aspect of body or the unconscious attempts to correct us when we are off course. If we pay respectful attention, the corrective can feel like a compass that guides our ship on its journey, but if we rudely ignore the gentle reminders, we might be rudely coerced to take note.

Our bodies provide information constantly. Fortunately for us, most of that information is picked up and acted on below our radar screens. We don't have to remember to breathe or to adjust our pH level. But some information – like painful joints if we are overweight – needs our attention and engagement in order to correct the situation.

One of the tasks of life is to learn how to care for ourselves. If we treat our physical and emotional selves as machines, or as wayward children or slaves that we have to whip back into place, our bodies are not going to love us for it. Our symptoms, to an extent, provide feedback as to how we are doing – messages that we are sometimes deaf to, or choose to medicate into silence. When the messenger knocks at the door and we ignore her for long enough, she may give up and we become stuck, or she could become furious or frantic, and break the door down, with catastrophic implications for our health.

Illness can be a signpost pointing in a direction we have been avoiding for years.

***

The ophthalmologist told me to rest my chin on the support and press my forehead against the bar to keep my head still. 'Look at the top of my right ear,' he instructed. Then he shone the astonishingly bright light into my eye. It was like looking into the sun – something I had been told as a child never to do. My body wanted to cringe away from this assault, my eyelids wanted to close. It was nauseating. But my will kept me sitting still, staring through the light in the vague direction of the doctor's ear.

'You know, you may be right,' he exclaimed. Those words burned themselves into my memory. I can even remember his tone of voice.

For some weeks I had been visiting the eye outpatient department at Groote Schuur Hospital, complaining about a cloud swirling in my sight. The eye specialist had reassured me that all I had was a couple of floaters, which were not in themselves a symptom of illness, and which are common in the general population. He had smiled at me benignly, noting that I was a medical student. Medical students tend to get all kinds of phantom or sympathetic illnesses as they work their way through the curriculum and the wards. This would happen to me too – an ear infection during the ear, nose and throat section of the curriculum, a urinary tract infection while studying urology, anxiety while participating in the day clinic as part of my psychiatry education.

But that day, concerned about my deteriorating vision, I had returned to be examined again, and the ophthalmologist had believed me. That was what it felt like: I had finally persuaded the expert that I was not making this up.

The ophthalmologist diagnosed an autoimmune disease. As an eighteen-year-old second-year medical student I had never heard of such an illness. It is familial in that it is carried by the HLA-B27 gene down the generations, but all my mother and sister had ever complained about was a bit of arthritis in the lower back. I was a reader, writer and a student studying beautiful histopathology slides through microscopes, and I was in danger of losing my sight.

My own immune cells, whose assignment it is to defend me against invasion by foreign objects and organisms, have somehow muddled their brief. They mistake the cells of my own body as foreign, rally the forces and attack the connective tissues in my eyes and spine. The inflammation that results causes pain and stiffness in my back and damages my vision.

A serious own goal. In fact, a series of ongoing own goals with no intervention from the coach. Why on earth would my immunity do that? Even now, thirty-five years later, we know very little about the autoimmune conditions. An unhelpful offering from my specialist was that a third of people with my illness get better, a third grumble on much the same with patchy vision, and a third deteriorate.

No-one could tell me into which third I would fall. No-one could advise me whether to prepare for a life of seriously impaired sight, or to carry right on as though this was just a minor pothole in an otherwise straight road.

At eighteen, I'd considered life a straight road. Not that it had been easy, but I thought I knew who I was and where I was heading. Born into a family who were not interested in psychology or religion, and who looked to science to provide answers, I had taken for granted that what was concretely in front of me was the raw material I had to work with to construct my life. The intangibles like dreams and soul held no meaning.

Disease provided a window, or rather a trapdoor, into a parallel reality – a reality based on the non-rational, which was nevertheless cohesive and imbued with meaning. If I had developed pneumonia or broken my leg, doctors, backed by science, would have rushed in and fixed me and nothing would need to have changed. But I was suffering from an illness that medicine barely understands. As a result, I was forced to look elsewhere to make sense of what was happening to me.

Initially, I did not do this. I attended the ophthalmology clinic and submitted myself to injections of corticosteroids angled behind my eyeballs and took the prescribed tablets and drops. These were sight-saving measures, although the treatment itself, ironically, can cause cataracts and other unwanted effects which obscure vision.

I carried on studying, evolving into a doctor, learning from tutors both explicitly and covertly how to become a medical practitioner. I studied the body as mechanism and as genetic construct and as chemical cascade. I learnt to take a family, medical and occupational history, to examine the body, to diagnose and to treat. Our class of just under two hundred students was taught that illness and injury are the failures of anatomical and physiological systems. We were steeped in the attitude that death is the enemy.

In those seven years, I learnt about an approach to the body that has had enormous impact on the wellbeing and life span of humans in the latter half of the twentieth century. Yet I could never shake off the feeling that there was something missing.

Over the next few decades after I qualified, afraid for my sight and in pain, I consulted a psychotherapist and a range of alternative therapies. I learnt from these teachers that there are many approaches that view disease as dis-ease, as the means our bodies use to alert us that we are out of kilter; I learnt too that accidents or 'bad luck' can be a way the unconscious tries to wake us up. I discovered that there might be something that life wanted from me that was neither ego-driven nor genetic, nor to be found in any rational manual. Wanting to track all sources of my condition, I became open to what I now think of as the poetry of the body – the way story and metaphor reveal themselves in the physical, emotional and spiritual self.

***

It is easy to misconstrue the body as being a machine. The way we fit together and pivot and hinge is awe-inspiring. Watching an orthopaedic surgeon operate with saws, glues and nails, one can be forgiven for thinking that a human body is a very sophisticated robot. Treating someone who has diabetes with insulin can look like supplying oil to an engine that keeps running out of this ingredient essential for proper functioning. Taking a pill to prevent conception can lead us to believe that we are in control of physiological processes that can be entirely understood through logic.

Yet there are aspects of disease and healing processes that we cannot take apart and explain as yet. One example is the placebo effect. We usually regard this either as an indication that the patient is a malingerer – that the symptoms are generated by their psychological state of mind, and that they have responded to a con trick – or as a nuisance, when studying how effective a new drug is. In trials that tested antidepressants,[4] the placebo worked almost as well as the actual drug. It begs the question why researchers are so keen to eliminate the effects of a placebo.

Another example is that women who have been trying to conceive for years without success, and then adopt a child and stop trying, not uncommonly become pregnant.

The focus of some researchers is shifting away from an approach which views the sick body as one whose systems have failed and which needs an external agent to restore health. They are starting to pay more attention to the innate self-healing capacities of the body and how they are either interrupted or activated, and whether and how this relates to ancient and indigenous practices. For millennia, humans have used story, ritual, talismans, voodoo, laying on of hands, going into trance, hallucinogenic drugs, herbs, 'energy', visualisation and vision quests, sacred places, dreams, throwing of bones, music, meditation, prayer, breath work, song, needling and scarification to protect and to heal. We also know that attitude and intention can make a difference in the healing process[5] – they are aspects of the overt or covert stories we tell ourselves about our illness and lives.

Measured in terms of numbers who consult, the success of alternative and complementary health practices cannot be merely accidental, nor anecdotal. Many mainstream practitioners regard these approaches as bogus as they usually do not stand up to rigorous testing. Indeed, many have not been adequately investigated, largely because companies who sell medicine are the ones who fund research.

I suspect that the popularity and anecdotal efficacy of alternative approaches to healing could lie in the power of symbol and story. Symbol as used in this book refers to anything we attach meaning to beyond what concretely exists: for example, an egg is a means of reproduction, but it symbolises many things – birth, rebirth, perfection, creation, hope, protection, fertility, to name the most common – and is employed in art, such as in Salvador Dali's paintings, and in rituals such as Pesach and Easter. A symbol, unlike a plus sign, cannot be pinned down as to its precise meaning, for we all bring slightly different and even pre- or non-verbal associations to bear. We know this from our dreams, where if we dream of an egg, we might experience a deep resonance, but be unable to express adequately the felt connection.

Even if we were to test alternative approaches to healing through double-blind, randomised, controlled trials – the gold standard of arriving at truth in medicine – this valuable tool might well prove to be inadequate. There is no ruler that can measure symbol, which in its essence can only point towards a constellation of approximate meanings, but can never signify something exactly. My experience, through my own illness, is that the body is both science and poetry, muscle and metaphor, chemistry and psyche.

> Even if the mind forgets,
> the skin remembers:
> the organs keep a record of their guests.
>
> Phillippa Yaa de Villiers[6]

In the twenty-first century, artists and scientists are working away at opposite ends of the table, observing, investigating, documenting. Both are attempting to find truthful answers using very different tools.

***

The development of the scientific method has shaped our age. It has helped us to differentiate fact from fiction. It can allow us to test our intuition and assumptions to see whether they hold true, and under what conditions they do. In medicine, science has helped us to identify unscrupulous practitioners and bogus treatments. It has provided a means for us to develop inspired strategies and interventions towards assisting the ill and injured and improving quality of life. In its pure form, science is curious and open-minded. In its corrupted form, scientists are in service to commerce, and might be more interested in profits, success and being right than in the truth, the health of individuals, or of the planet.

When serious practitioners of the arts – writers, artists, dancers, and composers – apply themselves to producing a work, they are also attempting to reveal what lies at the core of life. They are concerned with reflecting upon and provoking awareness in service to truth. Yet they employ fictions to do so: stories, representations, illusions.

Can scientists and poets talk to each other? Do these seemingly disparate approaches even speak the same language? The bridges that attempt to connect the lands of measurement and poetry have been rickety at best. Carl Sagan, the scientist and author, stated that he tries not to think with his gut[7], whereas Yeats, the poet, warns:

> God, guard me from those thoughts men think
> In the mind alone;
> He that sings a lasting song
> Thinks in the marrow bone.
>
> W. B. Yeats[8]

***

One of the many challenges of writing this book is what style of language to use. Poets use one kind of voice and scientists another, and each discipline often has serious difficulties with the style, affect, grammar and vocabulary of the other. Medical researchers tend to use objective, passive tense ways of expressing themselves in articles and books, and avoid words that spin off into multiple associations. Their brief is to be as exact as possible, to use words as scalpels to cut down to the bone of objective, verifiable truth. They go to inordinate lengths to write in such a way to keep themselves out of the picture.

Poets might keep themselves out of the writing, but they approach expression as a subjective enterprise. The words they choose evoke layered images, and through juxtaposing unusual words and phrases in unexpected ways they evoke metaphor and symbol, trying to see things anew, circling in on truth from a subjective, imaginative perspective.

As a writer of fiction and poetry, I identify with a poetic use of language, although I had to write scientifically acceptable prose when I worked in occupational health research. But the language of the laboratory is usually alienating and hard work to read.[1] I have to find a different way to set scientific contributions down. So I was pleased to discover that there are scientists who are writing popular science in a poetic language, like Antonio Damascio. We all need role models, and I will take him and author and neurologist, Oliver Sacks, and ask them to be my bodyguards and encouragers, and to sit by the door of my creative self. Above all, they are not to let in the wreckers: the strict critics, and those that speak in tongues of the passive tense.

Then, hopefully, a good time will be had by all.

***

Central to this book is an hypothesis – a term employed by scientists. An hypothesis, according to my Collins dictionary, is 'a suggested explanation for a group of facts or phenomena accepted as a base for further verification'. We all base our lives and decisions on explanations we conjure from a group of facts and phenomena. Ideally, like scientists, we test these theories out as we live, modifying or altering them when we come across contradictory results.

---

[1] A scientist friend pointed out that the same is true of some poems! I had to agree.

The hypothesis of this book is that the tools we learn in order to initiate, pursue and complete a creative project can also help us to live more awake, less anxious and more integrated lives. In the following chapters, I set down some facts and observations reported by scientists and artists, as well as findings of my own to support this thesis. This text proposes that the hypothesis is one worthy of testing to see whether it stands up to the truth. We can do this by carefully noting the results that emerge in the ongoing experiment of our lives.

I want to write a book about the body and psyche, about science and art, that my doctor colleagues do not dismiss, and that my homeopath and poet friends do not reject.

I am trying to talk to myself across the wide divide of the table.

***

2. Dancing to the Whistling

[The creative forces] have you on a string and you
dance to their whistling, to their melody. But in as
much as you say that these creative forces are in
Nietzsche or in me or anywhere else, you cause
an inflation, because man does not possess
creative powers, he is possessed by them. That
is the truth.

C. G. Jung[9]

Many cultures and religions – from the Buddhist belief in
karma and reincarnation, to the Christian commitment to God's
guidance – have promoted the view that human beings have a
predetermined purpose on earth.

An exhibition entitled *Museum of the Mind: Art and Memory
in World Cultures*, curated by the British Museum in 2003
displayed artwork by Osi Audu. Alongside was the following
text:

The Nigerian artist Osi Audu … has spoken
of creating objects as containers of memory.
He has in mind the idea that a sense of self
is constructed through memory; the self is a
projection forward of remembered experience
into present time. Each of us derives our selfhood
from our ability to remember. However, all is
not as it seems to Western ways of thinking.
Audu's inspiration is the Yoruba idea, which
he encountered as part of his own education,
that just before birth every ori (a word that can

mean both 'consciousness' and 'head') comes
to an understanding with God (Olorun) as to
the trajectory of their future lives. With birth the
detail of this agreement is erased from conscious
thought and concealed in the interior of the mind
within the inner head (ori-inu). Life is a struggle
to recapture the original plan and bring it back to
consciousness as a memory that can be worked
towards achievement. [10]

This example from Yoruba culture demonstrates a teleological approach (from the Greek *tele–* meaning end or goal, and *–ology*, derived from the Greek *logos*, meaning word, and subsequently study). It assumes there is an agency with a more inclusive perspective than oneself that knows better how one should proceed. This force can help guide us towards living a fully-fledged life. Some people call this entity God; others call it the psyche or spirit, others, the muse or daimon.

The psyche, according to the Collins dictionary, is the human mind or spirit. The name derives from the Greek word for breath or soul. The Jungian view is that the soul has no form and therefore needs the physical world through which to express itself, and give itself shape.

This world view is at odds with modern science, where the theory of evolution, brilliantly conceived by Charles Darwin and backed by tomes of evidence, shows that life arose out of random events and keeps changing due to mutations. Many scientists have used this evidence as proof that there is no greater force or guiding principle.

Yet most writers and other artists are very familiar with that moment when you slip through from the experience of the 'everyday' into the creative space where something else takes over. It is like entering a dream, where the person you usually identify as yourself becomes background, and other forces, other guides, slide in to help you or to direct your attention. Splendid ideas pop out of nowhere, connections emerge that you hadn't seen coming. Afterwards, you are nonplussed. I can't remember writing that, you think.

Guidance not only manifests while in the actual act of putting pen to paper, brush to canvas, or finger to string. When I began writing my novel *Once Two Islands* (Kwela 2007), motivated in large part by the themes, characters and concerns of Shakespeare's play *The Tempest*, a summer school brochure arrived from the University of Cape Town announcing a course on 'Rewriting the Tempest'! And when I set out to write this book on the overlap of the unconscious, the creative impulse, science and the body, Robert Bosnak, a Jungian analyst and teacher visited Cape Town for the first time, invited here on a lecture and workshop tour; his areas of interest are the unconscious, the creative impulse and the body. He is currently working with scientists in the USA in this interdisciplinary domain.

Jungians do not consider these happenings coincidental or random. They use the term synchronicity to describe concurrent events that seem related, yet in a non-causal way. Synchronous events are not uncommon, yet they are difficult to study. The psyche, or the unconscious, resists being pinned down, like the slippery edge of a dream upon waking.

Is making connections between non-causal events mere wishful or magical thinking? Does the mind seek and impose order where there is none? We know that large areas of the brain are devoted to making associations between inner perception, outer experience and memory, and that we might make mistakes when we correlate non-related events or memories.

The neuroscientist Changeux claims that the order we perceive in the world is a function of the brain itself. He claims that the human brain spontaneously creates mental representations that it tries to apply to an essentially meaningless reality.[11] He argues that this tendency of the brain to order reality is the basis for the creative endeavour.

Perhaps one day science will develop methodologies to understand, measure and plot the unconscious and the muse and all the forces that live through us. It is possible that one day we might develop one great theory that explains every phenomenon – scientific, spiritual and poetic – and which will put the arguments for and against to rest. I find it unlikely, in that we are stuck in the paradox that we must use the tool of the brain to examine itself. Yet both the poet and the scientist need to keep the door ajar to allow new ideas, and even each other, in.

***

Having embarked on this project, I am excited to discover that neuroscientists and psychologists have started to collaborate. When I was a medical student, we did not take psychology seriously. It was a vague subject founded on anecdotal evidence and taught by eccentrics. It had nothing to do with us; we were 'normal' students inhabiting a world that could be measured. The few hard facts we could relate to belonged to psychiatry, where drugs demonstrably changed people's behaviour.

In those days – only thirty years ago – society thought there was something weird about people who went into therapy. It was shameful to admit one was not coping and needed help. Therapy was for the mad and the unstable. In the emergency room, medical staff would label suicidal or anxious patients 'fruit loops'. Psychiatrists and psychologists were considered to be people who had a screw loose – strange people who might meddle with your mind.

The approach in other areas of medicine was generally straightforward: find the germ and kill it. Find the tumour and cut it out or zap it. But in the field of diagnosing and treating emotional suffering and thought disorders, the many conflicting theories made the discipline suspect.

Until fairly recently, scientific tools were unable to prise open the mystery of the subjective experience of inner life. Neuroscientists limited themselves to diseases that affected brain function like speech or movement. They deduced which areas of the brain were used for which functions from lesions at autopsy, by imaging the brain using computed tomography (CT) scans, or by surgically damaging parts of an animal brain. Scientists left investigating what governs the subjective experience of thought and emotion to psychoanalysts.

Neurology and psychology, approaching the mind from altogether different perspectives, were in the main openly critical of, and even hostile, towards each other. Now, with the invention of ways to study the working brain in real time through Positron Emission Tomography (PET) scans and functional Magnetic Resonance Imaging (fMRI),, scientists are able to penetrate terrain traditionally occupied by the likes of Freud and Jung. Mark Solms,[12] a neuropsychologist and psychoanalyst, has been investigating the neurological correlates of consciousness, the unconscious, and emotional life. Louis Cozolino, a psychiatrist,[13] has looked at changes in the occipito-frontal cortex (OFC) that correlate with changes in attitude and behaviour that occur during psychoanalysis. Candace Pert,[14] a neuroscientist, discusses the mind/body split as a cultural construct not supported by recent discoveries. Her research straddles the traditionally opposed paradigms of alternative and mainstream medicine, looking for a more inclusive and truthful science. The neuroscientist, Jean-Pierre Changeux,[15] argues that the neural connections involved in curiosity, motivation and reward are the same brain processes that underlie social drives towards rights to life, liberty and happiness.

These are significant beginnings. Understanding the links between seemingly mutually exclusive aspects of the brain, the mind, the body and the psyche, might help us understand each other, and even ourselves, better.

***

If the Yoruba are onto something with the idea that 'life is a struggle to recapture the original plan and bring it back as memory so it can act as a guide for living one's life', we might start looking for clues.

James Hillman, in his book *The Soul's Code*,[16] elaborates on the ancient Greek idea that before we are born we are each assigned a daimon, or a spirit, whose job is to guide us to fulfil a specific task on earth. The daimon is demanding, pressurising, and intolerant of us straying from our appointed task. She invokes all kinds of maladies and misfortunes to discourage us from wandering off, and rewards us when we 'get it', and get back on track, as it were. The daimon, not caring for verbal instruction, will resort to anything else to get our attention – boredom, depression, anxiety, curiosity, illness, accidents, forgetfulness, insomnia, blackouts, earthquakes.

Joe Goodbread, a psychologist, recounted in a workshop that he knew a chemist who was bored with his job, but did not have the courage to change what he was doing for the usual reasons – job security, perks, status. He was so bored that he lost concentration one day and blew his hands off. Without hands, he could no longer work in a laboratory and was forced to change vocations. He became a world-renowned mathematician and, despite not having hands, became more contented with his life.

The idea of the daimon is a teleological one. The daimon desires a specific direction, if not a particular end, and embodies an organising principle other than that of rational thought to indicate where we should be going. The influence of the guide is most evident in those children who are determined to follow a particular path from an early age, like the choreographer Gillian Lynne, and the musician Yehudi Menuhin and the composer Mozart, but Hillman suggests that we all have a guiding principle which reveals itself through force of character, chance meetings and synchronicities.

How else can one explain the vocation of the young man who told me that he was a translator for the deaf at conferences. I asked him whether he had learnt sign language because of a deaf member of the family, but he shook his head. He remembered standing in a school playground as a child. Through the fence, on the other side of the road, he saw someone using sign language. He said that he had no idea what they were doing, but was determined to know. He pursued this, despite his parents pointing out with concern that learning to sign would not get him a well-paid job. They were wrong. There are very few professional sign language translators, so he is paid well to work all over the world.

A friend, Ken Barris, recalls coming across the words dactyl, iamb and trochee when he was a boy. They stood out for him in a vast field of words, illuminated by something mysterious that drew him. He later became a poet and writer. Those words, it could be said, were cairns showing him the way to himself. He recognised something of his future self before he had any means to know what it was.

Eugene Gendlin,[17] philosopher and psychotherapist, suggests that both while creating a work of art and in living one's daily life, we use what he calls a 'felt sense' to check whether we are on track. He points out that when we make anything new in the world – art or the next chapter in the story of one's life – we often have a strong sense of how to proceed in order to complete it. Some aspect of ourselves knows where we are going, even though we have never been there before. We are constantly dipping into a somatically derived felt sense, which contains information collated not only from experience and expectations – which could only produce more of what already exists – but from a premonition of how the lived project or created piece will complete its unique shape in the future.

The psychoanalyst Helen Luke illustrated in her autobiography[18] the idea that our lives have strands of the symbolic and the teleological woven in throughout. She maintains that our early dream images recur in evolving forms, and that these motifs provide traces of our psychological development. In her case, the stone motif that first appeared in a dream when she was a young girl transformed from a milestone upon which she sat, through various permutations, ending as a dream of an enormous diamond in the sky just before she died.

In her book *An Experiment in Leisure*, the psychoanalyst Marion Milner observes: 'My mind's dominant concern, when left to itself, has been to achieve a conscious relation to the force by which one is lived. There seems to be something in my mind which is neither blind pleasure or pain-seeking, nor yet conscious reasoning; this something seems to be actively concerned with the truth of experience, and seems to express itself in terms of images, not arguments.'[19]

This premise of a thread or track or guide speaks directly to my experience as a writer. I had written poetry and short stories on and off since the age of seven, but soon after my first child was born, the muse seized me with intent. My immediate problem was that I had a beautiful, demanding, greedy, sleepless baby that I was hopelessly in love with, as well as a beautiful, demanding, greedy urge to write.

The timing was very inconvenient, but the imperative could not be ignored. I arranged two afternoons to myself each week and plunged without plot into my first novel. I did not know it then, but what I was really doing was growing my capacity for joy, suffering, and not knowing what on earth is going to happen next.

I was the kind of person who liked to plan things and to feel in control, yet here I was, sneaking away for two whole afternoons a week into a world where I was led by the snout of my pen wherever it wanted to go, sniffing out a trail of images and story. Learning to trust my impulse was liberating, even when it led down dark alleys where I was terrified to go. I learnt to trust the arrival of an unexpected character, or the development of a taboo situation or an event I thought didn't fit. I learnt to trust not to turn back too soon – that often enough if I persisted down the track of an annoying development for a few more pages instead of pressing the delete button, something would emerge that made total sense in the overall story. Threads would come together that I could never have constructed consciously.

What, exactly, do I trust? Some call it the muse, and say that the writer is a conduit for what needs to be written. Ursula Le Guin described writing the Earthsea series as a process of discovering something that was already there. Her job was to document it as accurately as possible. Some would call it intuition, or the daimon. Whatever it is, it is certainly not the rational mind, although, of course, the intellect has an important role to play, particularly in the research and editing processes.

I once met a successful international agent who told me that all good writers, writers who write best sellers, decide on an ending for their story, then plot their way backwards to the beginning. They know how things are going to wind up before they have even started. He wouldn't have agreed with film-maker Werner Herzog's comment: 'Coincidences always happen if you keep your mind open, while storyboards remain the instruments of cowards who do not trust in their own imagination and who are slaves of a matrix... If you get used to planning your shots based solely on aesthetics, you are never that far from kitsch.'[20]

Many books are written with the writer's ego largely in control. Generally, they do not speak to me, and I do not write that way. By extension, I am learning the value of relinquishing ego control in my life where necessary. The solutions that emerge from living in the moment, rather than planning a future outcome and living backwards from that fixed point, allow for some other mysterious influence, and prevent me from zooming, in a blinkered way, straight past what is perhaps the point of living.

*****

There are certain themes or motifs that have propelled my life story forward. They derive from images embedded at an early age, and which direct my attention to an underlying and sometimes contradictory pattern.

When I was twenty-nine years old, my first-born son had a freak accident, falling eight metres inside a public building. I found myself sitting helplessly next to his unconscious eighteen-month-old body in the neurosurgery intensive care unit. I could not even hold him, he was so badly injured. I did not know whether he would live or die. If he lived, I did not know how damaged he would be. I sang him his favourite nursery rhymes, and wept, and prayed. He survived, and, despite specialists announcing a doubtful prognosis, despite great personal difficulty, he has flourished. He is a magnificent human being, who chose to celebrate his twenty-first birthday by launching himself into the Gourits River Gorge on the end of a bungee.

I am not someone who believes that if you pray hard enough, or if you are good enough, there is a God who will answer your prayers. My son could well have died. Yet I began to contemplate that perhaps the secular approach to life did not explain events adequately. What I did experience, for the first time, was a handing over. I, the great achiever, the efficient fixer, the reliable doer, was totally impotent in the face of this disaster. Most of the people I turned to for emotional help and hope were unavailable. The specialist, whom I had worked with previously, was coldly factual and exceedingly brief from the other side of the bed. My husband and my parents withdrew, physically and emotionally, into their own versions of hell. Every minute was an agony of waiting, of not knowing what was going to happen next. All I could do was hand over the future of my son to something beyond my medical knowledge and sit alone, and sit, and sit, and wait.

A year later, I drew a picture of a fallen child under an enormous and sharp-toothed tiger fish, like those my father caught when I was young. An androgynous, conjoined figure was simultaneously supplicating and also preparing to attack the monster. Looking at the picture, it was difficult to tell whether the giant fish had pushed the child over, or whether it was instead protecting the fallen boy. It was also hard to say whether the fish was protecting the child from the fused parents, or which of the parents' strategies was the right one to get to their possibly threatened offspring.

I don't fully understand this turbulent image, but it still resonates with me. Over twenty years later I am still writing about falling in all its literal and metaphorical aspects. I am still investigating control and impotence, responsibility and victimhood, the events that shape one's life and the ways in which they do this. Over twenty years on, I am intrigued by the patterns that begin to reveal themselves during a life, and to what extent they are genetic and handed down through the generations, how much they are acquired from early experiences, or whether they display evidence of other forces that live through us.

Great Fish[21]

My father caught great fish, tiger fish.
He pulled their gleaming, dancing bodies
from the jaws of the Zambezi, severed
and salted their heads and strung them up to dry:
necklaces of death.

I felt them watching as I played
with trucks, earth and sticks,
amongst the mielie stalks;
their trapped, flat eyes
never leaving my back.

Sometimes I would chance a look
and see their rows of razor teeth
invite the blood that leapt in my finger
to touch them.

I could have touched,
seen my blood run.

I went inside at my mother's call,
washed the dirt off my hands and face,
sat still and straight at a white, starched table,
and ate their bodies.

It has taken me most of my writing life to come into a different relationship with this water creature, whatever it represents. The power of this poetic presence is as great as the scientific advantage of electricity through which I am able to use a computer.

Jung taught that image is psyche. Paying attention to the images that underpin one's life story provides a means to access and work with the force that lives through one – the themes and motifs of one's life, out of which we live and create. In Part Four we will investigate this idea further.

***

3. The Story of Our Lives

[We are] *stories* within stories within stories. We recede endlessly, framed and reframed, until we are unreadable to ourselves.

Ivan Vladislavic[22]

Every day people bring me their stories of pain, hope, frustration and fear. Every day they submit their physical selves to the inquiry of my hands, eyes and ears and of machines. Daily I must translate their words and bodies into facts, numbers and statistical probabilities, and advise them how to proceed.

Some people I meet in the consulting room are not in touch with themselves. They come across as victims of their lives. Many are stressed, anxious and depressed. They work long hours, don't have time to eat properly or to exercise, don't see much of their children, and drink and smoke excessively. They are overweight or they don't eat enough. They sleep badly. They wake up exhausted. When I ask them what they do for pleasure, they look perplexed or give half-hearted replies. There is a huge divide between who they want to be and who they are.

Ostensibly, we go to the doctor for information, advice and appropriate treatment. Often enough, what we really want is reassurance and a quick medicinal fix. Illness and injury are unwelcome disturbances. We want the doctor to get rid of these hindrances so that our bodies remain in the background and compliant. We are constantly trying to 'fix' our bodies, or else we hardly notice them at all.

***

The thin woman in her thirties came into my consulting room and sat down on the edge of the chair. 'I have this pain in my heart, doctor,' she said, pressing her palm against the left-hand side of her chest. 'It feels like fire.' She was worried she was having a heart attack. However, she had no risk factors for cardiovascular disease, and the pain was relieved by antacids. There was nothing to find on examination except for discomfort over the upper abdomen, and her electrocardiograph (ECG) and blood tests were normal. But she did admit to being stressed. She had financial concerns, and her home life was chaotic. She revealed that her husband was an alcoholic.

I explained to her that stress powerfully induces inflammation of the stomach lining, and that we should treat the indigestion. If it recurred, she would need to have a scope to check whether there was evidence of an ulcer or *Helicobacter pylori*, a bacterium associated with peptic ulcer disease. I told her that indigestion was her body's way of drawing attention to the toll her domestic stress was taking on her, and that she should get help. I offered the view that metaphorically, her heart was sore, and recommended AlAnon, the twelve step programme for family and friends of alcoholics, or, if she preferred therapy, a psychologist.

For the first time during the consultation, the woman looked happy. 'Oh, no,' she said. 'I don't need help. I know all about alcoholism. My mother died of it.' She smiled confidentially. 'My husband needs me. If I were not around, he would drink even more.'

This woman has a story about her life, as we all do. It is a huge plot point to have a mother who is an alcoholic. There are certain motifs to any human existence which set the frame of our time on earth – certain limitations and experiences that we can never divest ourselves of, and that we will have to live with for the rest of our lives. These are the the raw materials of our lives. Yet we do have freedom to interpret, subvert, embellish, and to use these materials creatively. I have heard it said of the poet Rilke that he did not want psychotherapy because he regarded his childhood trauma as the locus from which he wrote. He was afraid that therapy would rob him of this difficult yet invaluable source.

I don't believe that therapy can extract the thorn from one's side, but self-reflection is very helpful in making one aware of how that early wound informs and forms our entire lives. Without knowing something about the story that resides in your bones, you run the risk of the story living you, rather than you living your story.

***

Psychological theories interpret human behaviour. Two of the most influential thinkers based their theories on actual stories. Freud used the Oedipus myth to explain psychological development, whereas Jung taught the relevance of all myths in that they reflect the diversity of human behaviour.

In psychological theory, our lives incorporate plots through which we repeatedly play out our dramas, for example, the addiction to perfection and success, or the inability to see yourself except through the eyes of others, or mourning the lack of intimacy while keeping yourself out of reach. Myth typically represents the interactions and struggles between humans and the divine, and between the gods and goddesses themselves. Jung went so far as to say that the gods have become our diseases:

> We think we can congratulate ourselves …
> imagining that we have left all these phantasmal
> gods far behind. But … we are still as much
> possessed by autonomous psychic contents as
> if they were Olympians. Today they are called
> phobias, obsessions, and so forth; in a word,
> neurotic symptoms. The gods have become
> diseases; Zeus no longer rules Olympus but

rather the solar plexus, and produces curious
symptoms for the doctor's consulting room.[23]

I can hear the scientists shrieking at such a notion, as
I once did. But it is an astonishing image: Zeus residing in
the solar plexus, causing havoc. I think it is a measure of
impoverishment that, once we know that electrically charged
ions cause lightning, we laugh at those who believe in Thor. Yet
Thor's antics in the stormy skies speak deeply to the poet in us.

If our difficulties become too great, we might turn to
therapy in an attempt to resolve the tension. Analysis is the re-
imagining of the story of our lives. It holds the space open for a
battle of stories to take place. It values the symbolic life.

***

From the time humans pushed out frontal lobes, we have been
trying to understand and to communicate what it means to be
alive. During the past six hundred thousand years, humans have
developed an aesthetic sensibility. Wherever *Homo sapiens* has
gathered – around a fireplace in a cave or a dwelling, around a
waterhole or a bar counter, a conference or dinner table, around
preparations for ritual, worship or war, or around the birthbed
and the deathbed – we have told stories to each other to explain
how we came to be here, the purpose of our lives, and where we
go when we die. These stories are powerful, helpful containers
for our anxiety. They assist us to find purpose and meaning,
and they help direct our choices.

We are born into collective stories: the history of our family,
our culture, our country, our time. The woman with heartburn
entertains a story that both entraps and sustains her. Her body
is objecting to inordinate stress in the only way it can – through
symptoms. As a doctor I am suggesting to her that the way
she is living her story is not the only one. She requires both

courage and curiosity to venture outside the loop that both binds and contains her. It seems to me the psyche challenges us repeatedly in varied ways to alter our track. Symptoms are a form of feedback from the body that require a corrective to re-establish health. They are a means the body employs in an attempt to heal itself.

Changing your story can be terrifying. Adam Twerski, rabbi, psychologist and writer, has suggested that there is a 'Law of Human Gravity'[24]. He says that human beings will usually gravitate from a situation that appears more stressful to a situation that appears less stressful, meaning that we will only leave a stressful situation if the alternative is perceived to be less so. For my patient, changing the established dynamic with her husband feels more stressful than staying in it. We all have friends who won't change their lives, even though they might want to, and even though it is obvious to everyone else that change would be for the better. If we have lived long enough, we have all experienced a version of this predicament.

The story that you are immersed in can appear better or truer than any other version.

***

Human beings think and speak in words, images and stories. Our experiences form the basis of our world view, however skewed they might be. You can check this out very easily. Next time you meet a stranger, take note of the story that comes up immediately about him or her. We can even fall in love with someone we see for the first time across the room, or take an instant dislike to someone we have never met, but whom we can hear speaking in another room. We have a memory bank of associations linked to every single aspect of another person's appearance – the shape of the eyebrows and nose, the colours and clothes they wear, the accent and the tone of their voice, their complexion and expression, whether they make eye contact or wear make-up, their gait, their smell.

Practising medicine can be an effective antidote to making assumptions about people, because doctors meet so many people from all walks of life. The elderly, dishevelled person turns out to be a professor, the shifty character is merely shy, the charming man has given his wife a black eye, the man with gonorrhoea is not the one who is sleeping around, but has a girlfriend who is cheating on him, and the couple who look like mother and son are actually husband and wife.

Nevertheless, doctors can be as prone to false assumptions and prejudice as other people. When I was an intern in the gynaecology wards, a fifteen-year-old girl was admitted for an operation for excessive bleeding. She was Muslim, and her mother insisted on a doctor's certificate stating that her virginity had been breached by a medical procedure, and not by a sexual encounter. I don't know why a pregnancy test was not performed, but in theatre the gynae registrar found products of conception in her uterus. She was having a miscarriage.

Back in the ward, in front of medical students and other patients, the registrar attacked this frightened girl. 'What do you mean, you don't have a boyfriend,' he shouted. 'Do you have a girlfriend then, huh? Huh?'

It is one of the events that stand out in my training with rage and shame. I said nothing to this arrogant young man. Nobody stood up for the patient. Perhaps she had willingly taken a lover. Maybe she had been raped or been subjected to incest. I will never know what had happened to her. But I do know that the bad behaviour of the person supposedly in charge of her healing had just scarred her for life. The registrar had not only made assumptions about her pregnancy, he had victimised and publically humiliated her for a range of stories he tells himself about women, sex and Muslims.

***

Patients bring doctors their stories – about their lives and their illnesses. They also bring us their bodies: body as slave, child, robot, vehicle, machine, map of the unconscious. Body as terrorist, saboteur, hindrance, betrayer. Body as friend, guide, guard; as faithful servant, fragile membrane, resilient warrior. The body as process, repository of memory and trauma, of lineage, genetic pool.

One of the strengths of the medical model in which I have been trained is also a weakness, in that, in terms of disease, we are not interested in the personal details, or the subjective experience. There is a set of questions we ask to assist us with arriving at a diagnosis. We know from experience that most illnesses behave in predictable ways most of the time. The pain of gallstones is usually different in nature from that of a stomach ulcer, pancreatitis or gastroenteritis. The pain of migraine presents differently from sinusitis or a bleed in the head. Most illnesses can be diagnosed by categorising and correlating symptoms, even before an examination or investigations like blood tests, X-rays or ultrasound. Doctors ask directed questions: is the pain burning or tight? Is it sharp, dull or cramping? In medicine we don't want the whole subjective, perambulating story. The waiting room is full.

Yet disease occurs not only in the human body on the examination couch. It is present in the psyche and in the context in which the person lives. There is always a bigger picture or story attached to the ill or sore person seeking relief.

Sometimes doctors forget that. Sometimes, patients are not interested in investigating their own stories.

***

4. The Psyche Doesn't Speak English

> One great part of every human existence is
> passed in a state which cannot be rendered
> sensible by the use of wideawake language,
> cutanddry grammar and goahead plot.
>
> James Joyce[25]

I wrote the following poem for a friend who was suffering recurrent symptoms, and complained that she didn't understand what her body was saying.

Breaking the Code

My body's riddled through with flaws;
My dog's a whirling dervish.
At work I can't see out-of-doors;
My coffee's always warmish.

My face keeps breaking out in sores;
My dreams are full of catfish.
At night I clench and grind my jaws;
The psyche should speak English[2].

---

[2] Or any other verbal language.

The problem is, it doesn't. The language of the body manifests as symptoms; the language of the unconscious emerges as symbols. The workings of the psyche are deep currents, invisible but for the ways in which they form and inform the visible surface. Like geologists, we have to extrapolate from the surface disturbances and characteristics in order to determine the subterranean dynamics.

Jacques Lacan, a psychiatrist and psychoanalyst, whose interdisciplinary work drew on philosophy, linguistics and mathematics, proposed that a symptom was an embodied metaphor. The differences between simile, metaphor and symbol are as follows. In simile, we might say 'the moon is like a finger-nail' – the two parts are distinct. In metaphor we'd say 'the moon sails across the sky' – the parts are merged without our noticing, but the moon is still the primary object of attention. 'The moon rises in our blood' – the object takes on a broader and deeper association with an aspect of human experience, and we call this symbol. We find metaphors and symbols in poetry: 'All the world's a stage',[26] or 'Today I read entrails / over the low Drakenstein'.[27]

Lacan's view suggests that the twinges and flushes and snot of our bodies are a kind of poetry. Arnold Mindell, a physicist turned Jungian analyst, agrees. He says that unconscious information manifesting as symbols in night dreams is evident in our bodies during the day as symptoms, sensations and gestures. He maintains that our symptoms and our dreams are trying to wake us up to the fullness of our lives.[28]

Of course, if you suffer a heart attack, your body might be informing you that the way you have been living needs review. Or if cholera sweeps through a township, the authorities need to be brought to account for failing to ensure an adequate water supply. But what Mindell adds is a teleological, as opposed to purely consequential, view of life. He would claim that there is something drawing you to itself through your personal experience of illness. Attending to the medical condition at hand is, of course, important, but Mindell claims that if the underlying metaphoric condition is not processed, the information will recur, perhaps in another form, for example in a relationship difficulty. His is not a join-the-dots theory. Subjective experience is crucial, and investigating meaning can take unexpected non-rational turns.

***

A lecturer, whose living depends on speaking to lecture theatres full of students, developed dysphonia, or a hoarse voice. He saw a specialist, who sent him for tests, all of which came out normal. His physician recommended physiotherapy to alleviate his problem, but his condition did not improve. Working with me on the symptoms in a process way, he discovered that even outside the lecture room, he talked incessantly. His wayward larynx was trying to shut him up. On processing this further, he admitted that what he really needed to do was to write a novel that had been brewing for some time. In order to do this, he needed to be alone, and to be quiet.

He also admitted that he never felt heard as a child. Now his failing voice is making certain that he is not heard as a classroom teacher either. His task is to develop a different way of communicating what he has to say.

A woman who had travelled abroad developed a chronic, mild, smelly diarrhoea. Her symptoms were classic of an infestation by an intestinal parasite called Giardia. The treatment for this is metronidazole. Five tablets a day for three days would cure her, but she refused treatment, preferring to let her illness take its course. For eighteen months she had low grade symptoms on and off, and I was concerned for her, but still she was against taking medication. Then, overnight, her condition was cured.

Of course, it is possible for her body to heal itself, which usually takes longer than if one goes for the quick fix. What occurred just before this woman got better was that she recognised her tendency to 'leave the back door open' as she put it! The issue at stake was her ambivalence about her impending divorce, despite all the evidence that things were not reparable between her and her husband, who was living with another woman. Once she had resolved to bring the marriage to a close by instructing her lawyer to serve divorce papers on her husband, her diarrhoea stopped, and has not come back.

A mild-mannered woman had a red itchy rash on her scalp. She got a deep satisfaction from scratching until the rash oozed. Then she would keep scratching the scabs off. When I suggested she scratch something other than her own flesh, and carefully pay attention to what she was feeling as she did this, she snatched up a guava and began stripping the skin of the fruit off with her nails. Only when she got at what lay underneath did scratching become satisfying to her. She suddenly realised how furious she was with her husband, who worked a very long day. She felt he was avoiding her, but she rationalised her frustration away because he had a very important job. She wanted to tell him how she was feeling, and to try to get at what was underneath the skin of her husband's behaviour, but she was too afraid that approaching him would drive him still further away.

A scientist would argue that these examples are anecdotal, and do not withstand scientific scrutiny. Yet these outcomes are impossible to measure using scientific tools. There is enough anecdotal evidence for us to take seriously the theory that the psyche and the body have self-correcting strategies that go beyond the immune system, and that are aligned to the power of story and symbol.

It is arrogant to dismiss this aspect of illness. It denies us a fascinating way of getting to know ourselves better and to deal with core issues through paying attention to the physical difficulties that come our way, rather than stopping at popping a pill in order to get rid of them.

***

5. The Wounded Healer

When just a girl, I thought I'd fill the cup
Of those who choked with thirst, and never dreamt
Again, again, my frail veins would freeze up.

Siddiq Khan[29]

Recently, as I had been well for ages, I considered changing from a comprehensive medical aid to a hospital plan. First I did a whip-around of all the tests one ought to do at the age of fifty. Mammogram, bone density, thyroid, PAP smear, colonoscopy. It was an effort – time taken away from my lovely life to sit in waiting rooms, and to turn my flesh and bones and blood over to the probings of professionals.

My GP phoned me with the results. She told me that my bone density scan showed marked deterioration over the past eighteen months, and that I am hypothyroid.

My first thought: it's because of the bloody book. If I stop writing the book, everything will be fine. It's dangerous entering this terrain – things start happening.

My next thought: I either scrap the theory that your body is trying to talk to you, or the theory does not apply to me. I mean, all the people I know whose thyroids are under-active are rushing around, trying to juggle kids and work and deadlines, and beating themselves up because they feel exhausted. That's not me. My life is well-balanced. I have worked diligently to get to this point of equilibrium. I am engaged and curious, I am a good example to my patients, and – as a friend of mine once joked – I have passed all my therapy exams.

The inner scientist smirked: You see! Sometimes shit just happens! So much for your New Age mumbo jumbo.

I was reeling. My body had betrayed me. I took good care of her, and this was how she repaid me.

I told my GP that it wasn't fair, that none of this applied to me. She laughed, and told me that she checked herself for hypothyroidism all the time, as she was tired and sore and putting on weight. She said she wished she had hypothyroidism, so she could just take a pill and feel better.

I don't want to take pills. Not every day. OK, sometimes, when my backache is really bad, I will take something, but generally speaking, I am remarkably pill-free.

At work my colleague put his hand on my shoulder and looked into my eyes. He said, patiently, that taking a pill isn't that big a deal. My inner scientist agrees. She reminds me that I should be grateful.

I *am* grateful. My aunt had what must have been a severely under-active thyroid for years. She refused point blank to see a doctor. As a child I noted with horror, every time we visited her, how she bloated out, her voice turning to gravel, her movements increasingly slow and dull, her skin becoming coarse and dry, her legs elephantine. She eventually died of heart failure as an end stage consequence of the lack of thyroid hormone, the essential ingredient that maintains metabolism. She died because her fear of her body – or of doctors, or of taking medication – was greater than her fear of illness and death.

I thought of Emily Brontë, dying on a sofa aged thirty-nine, refusing to the end to see a doctor. I thought of Charlotte Brontë, dehydrating to death due to vomiting in pregnancy, and both John Keats and D. H. Lawrence wasting away from TB, and Robbie Burns dying of rheumatic heart disease, and Sylvia Plath, morbidly depressed, eventually managing to kill herself – all very young, all at the height of their creative endeavours, all dead of causes that are now treatable.

I couldn't think straight. Why? I demanded of my doctor. Why isn't my thyroid behaving?

We are getting older, she reasoned. Your thyroid is getting tired. It is not responding as it should. You must remember, she said, that we were not meant to live this long. We used to die of other causes long before parts of our bodies began giving way, giving up. And you have an autoimmune disease, which can affect the thyroid.

The word hubris came to mind. Eight years ago, the last time I was convinced I was doing really well, my whole life was pulled out from under my feet. My marriage ended, my adolescent sons both fell into deep but differing life-threatening trouble, my mother became very ill, I lost my job, and my health deteriorated. My sons and I all made it through intact, in fact better able to deal with life on life's terms, but when you are in the middle of crisis, it is terrifying. You don't know how the story will turn out.

Since then, I have felt wary of congratulating myself when things are going well. Instead I enjoy the respite and gather strength for the next wave of difficulties, or challenges. I try to be mindful when I am in the middle of difficulty, or when my life feels great, that the glass is usually both half full and half empty at the same time.

At this moment, all I can feel is water lost. Half-empty. Thyroid life force and bone minerals leaching out of my body, slipping through my grappling fingers, draining away. The poet inside is in mourning. She doesn't care about pills and potions. She wants to document this slow decline. She throws ash about and beats upon her chest, and accuses me of thinking that I am in control, of the hubris in believing that I can strike deals with my life, my fate. And of the pathetic conceit of thinking that if I am a really awake and conscious person, my body will be rewarded, or will reward me.

A hypothyroid friend who has been on medication for years postulates that there is something in the modern environment that is knocking off people's thyroids. There does seem to be an epidemic of the condition, and it is very likely that the interactive soup of unnatural chemicals we are exposed to daily – smog, tobacco smoke, preservatives, medication, drugs, colourants, flavourants, pesticides, etc. – has adverse effects that have not yet been documented. This could be one of the prices we pay for poorly monitored and overvalued 'progress'.

It is also possible that hypothyroidism is the shadow aspect or corrective of the Zeitgeist, or spirit of our times, which is fast-paced, instant, driven, gobbling dinner at the drive-thru.

For two days I have sat with this news, feeling vulnerable and afraid. I have not yet taken the medication lying unopened in the package in the bathroom. I am made to understand denial first hand. I am developing sympathy with those patients who are not interested in what I offer them in the consulting room from the other side of the metaphoric desk.

Also, I feel devastated, wanting to go to bed and weep into my pillow. And I want to laugh. To shriek with laughter. How ironic can this get?

This is a strange angel.

For a week or so I have been stuck, not knowing how to broach the next chapter. So, now, here it comes. It seems I cannot write about the body and illness, the psyche and art, from the outside, calmly and retrospectively, as the objective observer taking refuge in a place apart, reflecting back and reporting on what I have experienced and know. Instead, I am required to wade and fall into muddy waters, not knowing exactly where I am going.

I had a dream last night. I woke, and lay still a while, trying to catch hold of it, but it has gone. I need to pay attention now; I need to live the questions of my life and of this book on into the future.

It does feel unfair. It is outrageous that my body gave me no indication, no warning at all. Oh, except for hair falling out, now that I think of it. Long silver strands lying loose on my shoulders, the sofa, the floor. And inexplicable weight gain. And, since the diagnosis, I feel exhausted.

I take the first pill – Eltroxin 50 microgrammes. As I wait for it to take effect, despite knowing that it will take some time before I feel any different, I am very moved that this option is available to me. It is astonishing how humans, by applying their brains, have managed to identify this hormone and what it does in the body, and then discover how to manufacture it to assist those whose inner supply is dwindling. I am grateful to those men and women who go to work every day in laboratories in order to help heal me. It is a miracle: I can swallow this smidgen of substance – a mere 50 microgrammes – and it can save my life.

Acknowledging this medical advance, I am also going to bed to dream. May Psyche reveal herself. May she indicate what it is she wants of me.

***

> Body my house
> my horse my hound
> what will I do
> when you are fallen?
>
> May Swenson[30]

Five days later, and I am still feeling shaky and insecure. With this development in the narrative of my life, the ground has once again shifted under my feet. Fortunately, I am also curious.

So, here I sit with these symptoms, these symbols of the body, this dream, this unfinished story, this corrective we call hypothyroidism, which amongst other things is affecting the long term integrity of my bone strength.

The thing about the unconscious is that it *is* unconscious. We do not know what we do not know. Wherever we shine the light of understanding, in other places there will be darkness. Darkness contains what Jung called the Shadow, or the repressed aspects of ourselves – those gifts we are terrified to recognise, value and use; also those human traits we dislike and even despise in others, and deny in ourselves.

At the moment, I am afraid. The assumption that I can trust the process of my life has been repeatedly tested and found to be reliable, yet it is never easy to keep trusting. I want to be in control, I want to know where this is going and how it will all turn out.

I have a joke about this book, that when it is published it will be cheaper than a consultation. Embedded in this jest is the message: read this book and you won't have to see a doctor. Everything you need to know about your health and life you will find here. It is the message of the worst kind of self-help book. It is the message of fundamentalism, of arrogance. It says: life is simple. There is one door, and one key, and I have it. Now I am challenged yet again by the complex problem of illness. Also of ageing.

Illness is like a mini-death. It is a premonition of the overwhelming failure of the physical body, and makes us uncomfortably aware of our mortality. The scares surrounding avian and swine flu are reminders of the not too distant past when it was not infrequent for mere influenza to become pneumonia, which could end in respiratory failure or septicaemia.

Patients arrive in the consulting room wanting an antibiotic because they sneezed. They don't have time to fall ill, they say. They can't possibly miss work/an exam/a party on the weekend. They want to fix their bodies before they are even a little bit broken. Those with access to health care no longer have to go to bed with poultices and herbs and wait for the 'crisis', after which you either lived or died. But I think our bodies remember. We get fearful when we are incapacitated by illness or injury. Our bodies are part of the great cycle of the compost of life. We are all headed for the grave.

***

I am afraid that life is not as it appears to be. Another tiny shift, and everything again looks different. I cannot cling to this situation either, for this exact set of circumstances too is transitory. I must learn to live a dynamic existence in the midst of my need for permanence. The image of a surfer comes to mind – one who is skilled enough to ride the unexpected wave, who can be dumped without staying under.

I have often thought in life, similarly to when reading a story: I wonder what will happen next? Sometimes I am brave enough to pose it as an open-ended, open-minded question, but mostly I use it as a mantra, a verbal talisman to ward off evil.

So many strategies to fend off the void.

I am worried that my body is failing me. I don't want to be the patient. I want to be the doctor, the one in control, the intact one who dispenses treatment to ailing others.

How long will it take me to integrate what I know very well, that to be fully human encompasses every aspect of what it is to be human. I am a wounded healer, impaired in thought and body and action, blinkered in my attempts to apprehend the truth. It is the only condition possible, however much we aspire to perfection.

***

DAWN GARISCH

PART
TWO

Fear: The Guardian
with Two Faces

6. The Body is a Big Hook

> He lived at a little distance from his body,
> regarding his own acts with doubtful side-
> glances.
>
> James Joyce[31]

To be human is to be fearful. Fear is an appropriate warning mechanism that can save your life. When confronted by a real threat or danger, we can take appropriate action to avoid harm. Flight, fight or freeze are the fear-mediated responses of the animal world; in other words, run away, overcome the threat with force, or play dead. But undirected, displaced anxiety can undermine our lives and play havoc with our health. It can impede our capacity to pay attention to what is really happening, and can encourage rash and inappropriate action, directing choices towards outcomes that benefit neither ourselves nor the situation.

In the modern, industrialised world, now that we have dispensed with what, for millennia, were the usual suspects that dealt out death: lions and snakes, smallpox and gastroenteritis; now that we have controlled our environment with fences, air conditioning, and satellite tracking; now that we can easily summon help when we are in trouble with the assistance of cellphones, ambulances and helicopters; now that we have fire-fighters, third generation antibiotics and surgery, why are we so anxious?

Today I attended to two people who were afraid they were dying. The first was a woman who was very overweight. She said she had a tightness in her chest, pins and needles in her fingers and that she was finding it difficult to breathe. She

DAWN GARISCH

told me she was smoking more than usual due to the stress of the renovations at her home that had hit several snags. She had other risk factors for heart disease – raised cholesterol and hypertension, and her father had died of a heart attack in his fifties. However, the rest of the physical examination, her oxygen saturation, ECG and cardiac enzymes were all normal. The only finding of note was a fast but regular heart rate. Her symptoms subsided when I gave her Ativan, a powerful remedy for anxiety.

When I discharged her, despite my cautionary advice, she said she was going straight off to have a cigarette and a cup of coffee to calm herself down.

The second was a young man who had a feeling of discomfort in his chest. He could feel his heart racing and was finding it hard to breathe. He smoked thirty a day, was very stressed, and only drank coffee. Nothing else but coffee.

Both these people were suffering from panic attacks, exacerbated by large quantities of nicotine and caffeine. Both chemicals are stimulants that increase heart rate. In an already fast-paced society, it is fascinating that we choose to inhale and ingest chemicals that artificially speed up the metabolism. Some patients say they can't get going without a cup of coffee in the morning. Many people can't do without a drink to 'unwind' at the end of the day.

The body's needs are often different from our conscious agenda. Every now and then, out of the rushing rapid of our modern lives, our flesh and blood homes send out distress flares in the form of illness or injury. The bodies of these two patients were trying to force them to slow down and to take note.

It is a remarkable trait how alienated we are from our physical needs and stresses, considering the body is the only home we have other than the earth itself, another aspect of home we take utterly for granted.

***

Somewhere in the recesses of our minds we must know that we cannot escape what Lewis Hyde calls The Law Of Appetite.[32] Every living thing on this earth must consume in order to stay alive, and will eventually themselves be dined upon. Even though we have largely managed to banish polio and wild dogs, in the end we cannot avoid being eaten by death – by fire in the crematorium, or by worms in the earth.

During a lifetime we are presented with the problems of survival, meaning and limitation. Our attempts to resolve those three are embedded in our health, work, financial, relationships, creative and spiritual difficulties. We wish for our lives to be easy, free of constraint but, as M. Scott Peck reminds us in his book *The Road Less Travelled*[33], life is difficult. It is precisely those difficulties which make for an interesting story. Misfortune can bring out the best in us.

Yet we fear adversity and the unknown and insure on all fronts against disaster. We do not trust our bodies or our lives and we worry about things before they have happened and that will probably never happen. We cannot sleep at night for fear of what tomorrow might bring and we make decisions based on predictions of the worst outcome. We think the unconscious is out to get us or that we are victims of our lives. The human default position appears to be anxiety.

Depression and anxiety are on the increase. We now understand these conditions as part of the same disease. A psychiatrist once told me that this disease will soon be the most prevalent illness of our time.

In my line of work I meet many people who are fundamentally anxious. Their anxiety is often free-floating, and can settle on anything. They constantly and unconsciously seek a hook to hang it on. They seem to think that if they can say, This is why I am anxious, it will validate their fear and give them some relief. The body is a great big hook, with its mysterious inner workings and invisible germs, its twinges and lumps. On several occasions I have had young people with infected throats come to me, concerned about cancer. What's this lump, doctor? they worry, prodding their enlarged cervical lymph glands.

I spend at least half of my time at work educating and reassuring patients. Doctors and other health practitioners are there mostly to make you more comfortable and less anxious while your body does the work of recovery. Occasionally you might need a little more assistance – in the form of an antibiotic, for example – and sometimes symptoms might flag a more serious condition. Mostly you can help yourself recover by taking time out, resting, drinking enough water and eating well.

***

A nurse pushed a woman in a wheelchair into the procedure room. She had difficulty getting from the wheelchair onto the bed, because, she said, everything was spinning. Then she vomited and started to cry. She said it felt as though she was dying. I treated her nausea, then took a history and examined her to confirm my diagnosis. She had labyrinthitis, where the organ of balance in the inner ear sends the wrong information to the brain, and the world wobbles and swerves. Viruses can cause this, as can a loose otolith. She was very alarmed, so I took extra care and time explaining the illness. When I had finished, she looked at me anxiously and said, 'Yes, but what is *wrong* with me, doctor?'

Briefly I was frustrated with her for not listening. Then I realised that it was a good question. Paying attention to her, it was obvious: labyrinthitis was not her biggest problem.

***

7. The Valley of the Shadow

I move through our rooms
A somnambulist or deep sea diver
With leaden boots, turning off
The lights, lowering the blinds,
Ensuring that the doors
Are locked, the shutters bolted.

Michael Cope[34]

A South African artist, Zhane Warren, has made a piece entitled 'My Fears'. It consists of a cardboard box that contains two hundred and seventy-six A4 sized pages of rice paper. On each is printed a sentence, beginning 'I fear ...' Two hundred and seventy-six different fears on a stack of edible paper!

It is a powerful piece – the volume and weight of fear, the layers and range, the obsession and focus of fear, the compounding of fears with no relief. The time fear consumes, just to wade through the compelling list she has detailed for us all to see and note and recognise. We speak of being consumed by fear, yet her work depicts fears we can consume, take into our bodies – fears becoming flesh and blood. The urge was almost irresistible; once I had read that the paper was edible, I wanted to taste it, chew and lick it, swallow it down along with the fear.

Do fears come from inside or outside? Are they monsters, bogeymen and tokoloshes that hide under the bed with evil intent? Do we feed ourselves a diet of fear laid out like a feast in the daily papers, with an extra big helping on Sundays? Or are our terrors instilled in us from an early age, and now reside within us, ready to take us down at the slightest provocation?

In his book *Why Good People Do Bad Things*, psychologist James Hollisi[35] shows how a child learns to repress aspects of himself that the adults around him do not like. These unmediated inhibitions make him socially acceptable to his parents and community, but many of the natural drives that comprise being human – like fear, anger, desire and need – are not allowed appropriate expression, and are driven underground. These split-off features of ourselves form aspects of Jung's concept of the Shadow. Not surprisingly, these very fragments of himself that a child is taught to be afraid of and to deny, are also the parts the adults in charge fear about themselves.

Suppressing these drives does not make them go away. They can return repeatedly as disturbances in our behaviours and relationships, and in physical symptoms. The natural expressions of fear, anger, desire and need can get subverted, even perverted, when they are not permitted normal outlets. Our society is riddled with anxiety, violence, sexual abuse, corruption and addiction.

'Bad things' are committed by people who think of themselves as 'good'. We are all split beings, engaged in an ongoing, internal civil war.

***

Not surprisingly, we want to avoid the sensation of fear. When we are young, we put what Hollis calls anxiety management plans in place. We adopt these strategies in order to feel better. Unfortunately these habits we employ can be a trade-off with long-term disaster. Comfort eating, fixed routines, substance abuse, social withdrawal, belligerence, and being hypercritical or perfectionist are examples that can all provide a measure of security in the short term, but provide poor frameworks for negotiating the complexities of life, health and relationships.

A patient, whose chest was wet with tears, told me she was not coping at work. All she wanted from me was something to help her get back to her desk. Taking time off, she insisted, was out of the question. It turned out that her life partner had left her a year ago. Her anxiety management plan was to throw herself into her work.

Her exhausted body had stopped her in her tracks. From her story, it was clear that she needed to attend to her grief, but she was having none of that. She refused everything I offered – leave, therapy, hospitalisation, antidepressants. All she wanted was quick-fix medication to calm her down and to help her sleep so that she could get back to the deadlines. A telling word: deadline.

I recognised that she was unable to be on her own side, and gave her a short course of medication to help her feel calmer and to sleep, repeating my recommendation that she take time out and go into therapy to reconsider her life. I asked her to come back and see me, but she did not. I have wondered what happened to her. Sometimes people only pay attention when they are so anxious and exhausted that they have a car accident, or other major trauma. They are then forced to stop and face the terror of the void.

***

One interpretation of the story of the Garden of Eden is that before Adam and Eve ate fruit from the tree of the knowledge of good and evil, they had no awareness. They were at one with God. Instead of remaining obedient, however, they were curious, and bit into that irreversible apple. The result was awareness, and with awareness came banishment from the state of at-one-ness, or Eden. With separation comes consciousness, which brings with it apprehension – the word 'apprehension' meaning both the faculty of comprehending and understanding, and also anxiety about what could happen in the future.

Awareness allows us access to a bigger picture. It also forces onto us the contradiction that as individuals and as a species we are on the one hand important and valuable, and on the other we are as nothing, existing for a brief moment in the huge drama of the universe. We live between two darknesses – our lives are brief parabolas into light, out of the void and back into the void, out of the earth and back into the earth, out of spirit and back into spirit.

We tend to see birth as a positive event, the miracle of a new being arriving essentially out of nothing. A whole new and discrete person, made in the image of the parents, grows slowly from a baby who is totally dependent on her caregivers for her survival, into a child aware that she is not at one with her parents. She becomes a separate being, capable of her own independent thoughts and actions. Like God in the Garden of Eden, the parents are not always pleased with this development.

On the other hand, we tend to experience death as a negative event, the tragedy of a well-established character disappearing into nothing. We mourn the loss of our loved one, and struggle to grasp that we can no longer ring him up nor drop in to see him. The dead person has stepped away, back into the void; disintegrating back into the earth, merging back into God.

Those things that give us indescribable pleasure in life are usually felt as brief moments of at-one-ness, a merging into bliss, into another, or into the fullness of life. Boundaries dissolve and we are back in the haven of Eden. Conversely, those times that evoke terror and deep depression are those where we feel as though all support and certainty has fallen away, and we are left unutterably alone and afraid. We strive for at-one-ness, and we try to avoid the void. Yet they exist side by side, like birth and death.

***

The neurophysiologist J. Z. Young[36] notes that living things are remarkable in that they have developed systems that can withstand the ubiquitous tendency for all substances to merge back into the surroundings. This means that, while we are alive, we have systems in place to stop ourselves from rotting. People, even health consultants, forget that. They mistrust the body's innate healing capacities, and want to rush in and fix something before it has had a chance to fix itself. There is a bad joke amongst back surgeons: Operate soon, before it gets better.

Often enough the body can heal itself of acute conditions – and we can assist this if we are kind and nurturing, as one would be to a child. There are also many conditions that used to cause death which we can now cure or ameliorate. Modern medical practice has come to be synonymous with control of natural processes through medication and surgery.

A short while ago humans had little influence over conception, birth, illness and death. The modern way is to control these events – in part to avoid suffering. The Caesarean section is an operation originally performed to save the life of the child, the mother, or both, and yet some women choose to have Caesarean sections because they say they are afraid of pain. Yet they know that surgery involves pain. On the other hand, labour is unpredictable in terms of the severity of suffering and how long it might take. Cut the baby out, and you can be back in the ward before lunch.

There are patients who take pain killers in case they get a headache, and those who want an antibiotic at the first sign of influenza.

None of us welcomes suffering, but even minor discomfort can trigger disproportionate anxiety. I tell my patients who need to lose weight to expect to feel a little hungry occasionally. People generally prefer to feel over-full than slightly hungry, and over busy than at a loose end.

***

A young man was waiting to see me in the procedure room. He suffers from panic attacks, and said he was too afraid to go to sleep because he was worried he would die. It is a common time for anxiety to rear up: the moment one drops off to sleep, there is a letting go of control, a real sense of 'falling' asleep. For someone who is very fearful, this sensation can feel unbearable.

I suggested that he try to talk himself down, rather than wind himself up. After examining him, I asked him to do a reality check and confirm what was obvious – that he was a fit and well young man who was not going to die in his sleep. He was unable to do so. Logic is often a frustratingly inadequate tool.

Anxiety can be paralysing, exhausting. Medication can provide respite from unrelenting tension. I tell fearful patients that taking anxiolytics for a short period of time can be helpful if they regard these drugs as crutches while their emotional legs are getting better. The word anxiolytic is derived from the Latin word *anxius*, related to *angere*, meaning torment. *Lysis* comes from the Greek word for loosen. An anxiolytic, poetically, is something that loosens torment.

At the same time as prescribing a pill to loosen torment, I encourage an anxious patient to observe whether his body is drawing urgent attention to unresolved difficulties. The fear of dying, for example, is not necessarily something to take literally. It can be a powerful indicator that something needs to end.

***

Many patients avoid asking for help. Their anxiety management plan is a story that says they cannot trust anyone else, and that they can do it on their own.

A tall, thin and attractive man was brought to the clinic by his girlfriend. He sat and stared at the ground for some time without speaking, other than to tell me that he was stressed. I remarked that he looked depressed, and that he appeared to have lost weight, to which he nodded. I told him that we all go through difficult times, and that we all need assistance at some point in our lives. I reassured him that there was plenty of aid available if he was ready to ask for it, from therapy to medication to self-help groups and phone-in counselling. He turned each suggestion down, saying that he needed to work it out by himself. I asked him how long he had been trying to do it on his own, and he admitted that it had been years.

I turned to the girlfriend and asked for her view. She said that her boyfriend had mood swings, and became aggressive, and even hit her on occasion. The man cut in, saying that she provoked him, whereupon I challenged him, saying that nobody can make you get violent – that was his responsibility entirely. For a moment he looked as though he was going to hit me, then he stormed out of the clinic. I encouraged the woman to get help herself, including an interdict. Yet she insisted she was fine – that it was her boyfriend who was the one in trouble.

Asking for help is an act of vulnerability, humility and trust. It requires loosening your grip on the way you have always done things. It means being prepared to relinquish the illusion of control and to allow another in.

***

Wherever possible, we have eliminated all bugs, vermin and predators that intrude on civilised life, or we have confined them to nature reserves or zoos. We have managed to render all organisms largely harmless to our way of life, from streptococcus and rats, to snakes and lions. The irony is that once we have managed to get rid of them all, we will have a lot to worry about. Jonas Salk, who pioneered the polio vaccine, pointed out that if all insects disappeared from the earth, within fifty years all plant and animal life on earth would die. But if human beings were eliminated from the earth, within fifty years the planet would have recovered from the devastation we have wrought.[37]

Fear of nature interleaves with the fear of loss of control and fear of the void. When frontal lobes made an evolutionary appearance, humans benefited from what are termed 'higher functions' – faculties of reason, discrimination, restraint and planning, and the capacity to develop culture. Unfortunately by reason of our reason, we have begun to see ourselves as more advanced and therefore more important than animals, which function reflexively in the main. Humans see themselves as superior to, or different from, nature. Even our language reflects that. When we talk with concern about 'the environment', we leave ourselves out of the picture.

The biblical injunction that man has dominion over animals and the earth has fed our perception of human sovereignty, or primacy, as has scientific enquiry. Nature, seemingly out of our control, even dangerous to us (as are we, often unknowingly, to nature), needs to be conquered and tamed by ownership and agriculture, insecticides and toilet cleaner, medicine and surgery, fences and guns, dissection and analysis, weather forecasts and genetic manipulation, landscape gardening and battery farming.

Julian David likens nature, and the earth, to a feminine principle of a goddess who does not function by the logic of power, but by the binding force of Eros:

> When people started to enclose the land it was
> as if they took a piece of the ancient goddess
> and dared to call it theirs … Instead of weaving
> back and forth over the skin of the goddess,
> hunting her animals, making painted cathedrals
> in the caves of her womb, gathering her fruits,
> dependent for every breath on her good will, they
> were going to take her prisoner, parcel her up,
> distribute her amongst themselves, make

her the sinew and muscle of their lordship. They
took her sacredness and ... transferred it to a
male god, who then transferred it to them... And
... it dawned in someone's mind a blasphemous
thought – that perhaps one need not worship the
goddess any longer, but conquer her. And when
they find that it actually works, and that they have
the power of the gods in their own hands ... and
that within a mere ten thousand years the world
is transformed and brought also to the brink of
its own destruction, 'what', they must ask, 'has
gone wrong?'[38]

We further embody the split between people and nature by
valuing the brain more than our physical selves. We often think
of the mind as rational, with the body as nature out of control,
with all its urges, smells, reflexes, excretions and secretions, and
desires. Our flesh and blood homes are even seen as disgusting,
and must be kept in check with a range of products.

Bacteria are everywhere. Right at this moment, there are
about four hundred on either one of your hands. It has always
been so. It is natural. It is nature. Watch any crawling child,
and notice how often he puts his hands and other objects into
his mouth. Not only is he learning about his environment by
tasting it and examining it with his lips and tongue, he is feeding
himself with a huge range of micro-organisms, thereby waking
up his immune system. Bugs often live in essential harmony
with organisms around them, including us.

Yet advertisers warn us to 'kill all known germs dead'
by buying their anti-bacterial soaps, cleaners and antiseptics.
Understanding how hygiene prevents illness has revolutionised
medical care, but our fear of bacteria, paradoxically, can result
in disease.

Probiotics were largely unknown a decade ago; now
they are the new wonder treatment for many problems, from
constipation to diarrhoea to recurrent viral infections. Probiotics
are germs. A drug rep told me the other day that there is a new

probiotic on the market for babies born by Caesarean section. We have known for some time that certain bacteria are necessary for normal gut health; now researchers have found that being born through the vagina inoculates a newborn with appropriate bacteria which colonise the baby's intestines for good digestive and immune health.

Our consumer culture has pulled off the most incredible scam: sell people household and body disinfectants and antiseptics to sterilise their environment, then sell them bacteria in sachets and capsules as a medicine essential for health.

***

Insecurity stems in part from our inability to control and predict the future. There is a lot of money to be made from this kind of fear, from fortune-telling to the unscrupulous 'Lifescan'. If you are wealthy enough (no medical aid is ever going to pay for this test, and no self-respecting doctor is ever going to order it), you can arrange to have an MRI scan of your whole body at your local private X-ray department. The idea is to pick up abnormalities like plaque in a coronary vessel, or a pre-cancerous polyp of the colon, or cyst in the ovary, or tumour in the brain before it has presented in the body with symptoms.

For the cost of a second-hand car, you have a whole body scan that infers that you are totally free of disease – for that precise moment in time. Until you start worrying again about what new disease has taken root just after the scan was done, and is lurking unseen, unfelt, in the horror chamber of your physical self.

Yet insecurity does not only concern the psychological problems of inner life. To feel secure, we also need to feel that we have good footing in the world.

Our political, economic and sociological arrangements frequently seem counter-intuitive. We must suspend our better judgement in order to accept much of what has become 'normal'.

We spend hours in traffic jams, cut down trees to flood the world with junk mail, drink artificially-flavoured, sucrose-saturated water, wreck our backs wearing high heels, buy cars that cost more than houses, and build houses for cars. We buy into the manipulations of corrupt politicians and bankers, accept the obscene and ever-widening gap between rich and poor, expect new cell phones every year, buy mass-produced clever but trite gimmicks and gadgets which then fall out of fashion and into the rubbish bin, design superfluous packaging that costs more than the food or drink it contains and which we then throw away. We throw away, throw away, throw away as though the earth can endlessly receive our exponential accumulation of waste. Our perceived and transient need for some fad trinket might have meant long hours of hard work for disempowered people in poor working conditions for shockingly low pay.

For our economy to work, we are encouraged to buy into avarice and waste. We know that another pair of shoes or a bigger car is not going to solve the problem. It might even make things worse if we buy the car on credit. We know we are conning ourselves. A friend describes the world economy as the biggest Ponzi scheme ever invented. We are continually borrowing from natural resources without any intention of paying back what we owe. We are being sold an unsustainable, unethical system that results in our soiling our own nest.

The way we live makes for a shaky foundation. We put our full trusting weight on what might turn out to be veneer. Veneer is that thin covering we take for the real thing. Oak veneer is a cheap way to achieve a pleasing finish to furniture in a world where hard woods are no longer abundant. But scratch below the surface, and you will find chipboard. Given a flood, or hard knock, chipboard will break and fail.

We need to agitate for and promote good governance, so that civic life is supported by policies that promote sensible practices in food security, environmental integrity, public health, crime prevention, education, energy, health and welfare.

Yet we are not inclined to scratch too deeply. When a colleague at work asked me what I was writing and I told her, she gave a worried smile. 'That sounds soul-searching,' she exclaimed. 'Are you sure that's good for you?'

Our heads are so deep in the sand, it's no wonder we are having difficulty breathing.

***

8. Of Detectives and Gardeners

This much is all we have:
shadows gathering,

fugitive grace
and the deep body as our penumbral space.

Ingrid de Kock[39]

My back is sore. I have been working – alone and hard – at the computer, and I want somebody's hands on me. What I want is to relax in someone else's care – to give my physical self over to kind hands. It is a gift to my body. So yesterday I went to someone who practises shiatsu and who has a good reputation.

What I keep forgetting is that healers want to fix things. Whenever I go to someone for any kind of therapy and I give them my medical history, I can see their eyes light up. They adopt an heroic look. It doesn't help to explain that, having lived with a chronic condition for thirty-three years, and having spent a fortune on various therapies in search of cure, I have come to the point where I want to give up on the goal of healing.

I am fortunate that the eye manifestations of my condition appear to have burnt themselves out. I would rather have backache than lose my central vision.

Now that the consequences of my illness are not so severe, I want to accept myself as I am, with all my flaws. I want to relieve myself of the burden and expectation of having to get better. As a doctor and a patient, I want to embrace the fact that thinking you can fix everything is a denial of the limitations of physical reality, which includes death. But as I listed my physical and physiological imperfections, I could see the shiatsu practitioner rising to the challenge. I felt myself sigh inwardly. It is almost impossible to tell someone in the healing profession that you don't want to be fixed. I would then sound like the worst of my patients. We would stare at each other, each with the same thought-bubble about the other – she's in denial.

***

The art and science of healing is like the difference in approach between a gardener and a detective. Good gardeners know that the life force needs tending with respect, patience and care, and that a garden is a dynamic process that cannot be planned entirely in advance. They accept sickness and death as a part of nature. The life force does not favour the rose over the aphid, the arums over the porcupine, the potato over the blight.

Gardeners work slowly in tempo with the seasons, using their knowledge of the soil, plants, insects, birds and disease to foster life. Gardeners know the limits of their capacity to control, and trust natural processes to do a core part of the work.

Detectives use different tools. They have a mystery to solve. They gather clues to track the culprit down. They are quick, efficient, and focused. There is a solution, and time is of the essence. If necessary, the detective will apply pressure to get what she wants.

You don't want to adopt a gardening approach when resuscitating a patient. On the other hand, the attitude of the detective is unhelpful when someone is grieving.

The best healers combine both approaches and pay close attention to all aspects of the process. They listen carefully to what the afflicted is saying. Right now, I don't want to be dissected or diagnosed or processed. My body is probably littered with exciting clues, but at present, I just want to be accepted, held and nurtured. That is healing enough.

***

9. On the Fear of Failure

i have one eye full of dreams and hintentions
the other is full of broken mirrors
& cracked churchbells

i have one eye full of rivers and welcomes
the other is full of flickers and fades

Seitlhamo Motsapi[40]

I am faced with failure, of not being good enough.

I did not get the writer's grant, which would allow me time off to complete this manuscript. At the Cape Town Book Fair, I met up with the director of the association that administers the grant. He told me that it had been a close thing. Most of the judges on the panel liked my writing and the subject matter. The objection, he said, was that some judges were doubtful that the project qualified as non-fiction. He encouraged me to reapply, which is what I will do, only this time I will bump up the science and autobiography for the purposes of the application.

The irony is fabulous: the judges have decided that my investigation into the methods artists and scientists use to evaluate truth – which includes the imagination – is not non-fiction! Non-fiction, according to my dictionary, refers to 'writing that deals with facts and events rather than imaginative narration'.

What a conundrum. Maybe I should give up right now, and stick to the boundaries. Go back to fiction. Boundaries are good. They let everyone know where they are.

Or I should be encouraged by E. L. Doctorow, who said several decades ago that there is no such thing as fiction and non-fiction, there is only narrative. Or the poet, John Keats: 'I am certain of nothing but the truth of imagination and the holiness of the heart's affections.' Or Einstein, who felt that imagination was more important than knowledge.

Nevertheless, when I did not get the grant, I went into a minor slump, as well as wanting to burst out laughing. My notion of 'angels stampeding to help me', which arrived on the opening pages in full writing flight, I decided to keep and not edit out, as I found the image hilarious and hopeful, despite an attendant squeamishness at the quaint narcissism. Now it is just embarrassing. Am I deluded about the potential help provided by Psyche, available to anyone on taking a determined step in the direction of desire?

Yet the call for applications for a grant set this huge project in motion. That I do not regret. That is just what I needed. So, on I go. But how? Increasingly I feel the need to take uninterrupted time off my demanding day job to complete this book.

My son, who has believed in this project from the outset, suggests that I should be my own benefactor. I should award myself a grant out of my access bond. I might well have to do that. Writing non-fiction turns out to have different demands from fiction. I have completed a first draft of nine chapters, with a hundred pages of scrambled notes, and there are ten books teetering next to my bed on relevant topics. I am currently reading about the neuroscience of consciousness and about product branding, also the poetry of the body. The track I am following has changed, chapters I had planned have been deleted, new ones have taken their place. Writing this book needs focus, time, a vibrant energy. Some mornings I wake up with a whole chapter in my head, and then have to go to work. I jot reminders down, and hope it will be enough to jog my memory when I eventually get back to that thought, perhaps only in several months' time.

I need a patron of the arts, no strings attached. But that gift is rare. Grants fulfil that function, but most contemporary patrons of the arts are essentially no different from those of days gone by. They want their pound of flesh. Previously in the western world, the artist received assistance from the church or from the wealthy and, in return, was required to paint or compose subject matter in honour of the patron.

In modern times, many a young person with an artistic bent who wants to earn a living from art is absorbed into the advertising and media world, where he is in service to the product, and thereby in service to the pocket of the owner of the brand. Graphic designers, film makers, copywriters, musicians, art directors, composers, actors, are employed to apply their considerable talents to manipulate the public into wanting to buy things that they don't need, or don't even want.

Scientists as artists, using their imagination and knowledge and skill in order to invent – what Changeux[41] calls tinkering in the neuronal workspace – are often in this position too. Private companies, state institutions and universities are the patrons who can afford to finance research projects. University laboratories are subsidised by the government, but they are often assisted with private money too. Private investors want financial reward for doing so. Scientific research ceases to be open-minded and open-ended – it has a specific goal: a product that will make the financiers even wealthier.

***

Many people I meet say they would love to write. Or they tell me they used to dance, paint or sing. They once had a guitar, a piano, or a kiln. They would love to take it up again, but …

While running workshops on creativity, I have observed how afraid people are to express themselves artistically. The desire is often there, but something comes up to stop them.

What if I begin and make an 'inept' movement, or 'ugly' mark or sing out of tune? What if the 'wrong' words emerge, or if I do not have the skill to execute my exact intention? What if I make a fool of myself, and everyone is watching?

It can be very challenging to step into our creative lives. It is an unfortunate human tendency to take imagination, a cornerstone in the creative act, and to subvert it, using it as a weapon to cripple ourselves instead. We imagine our humiliating failure even before we have put pastel to paper, or else we imagine fame and fortune while writing a novel, then, when it does not even get published, we use that as a reason to retire to the sofa in front of the TV.

Employing a professional to tell us what to do and how to do it can ease the terror. Technical skills are very helpful, and role models can encourage us by demonstrating that it is possible to achieve one's goals, but no-one can teach us how to find out who we are and what we have to say in our own unique way.

***

Back at my desk, I have decided: I will face the terrors of the creative void, financial insecurity, imperfection, disapproval, failure and success. I will find a locum to take my place at work for two months in order to finish this book.

***

10. Rhyme or Reason – Fear's Role in the Brain/body

I have stood in the kitchen giving up on it,
betraying it, betraying you,
giving it to the wind, to the field in front of us,
to the fallow ground;

saying: nothing compels me,
it is too much for me,
too far out and beyond me –
.....
What do I have to do
to get through to myself
what do I have to do?

Joan Metelerkamp[42]

We need to know more about fear, and how it operates in the brain/body, so that we might begin to take steps to decrease its negative impact.

Just as there are distinct facial expressions for the emotions, there are different physiological profiles in the organs that accompany the emotion. We call these physiological profiles feelings. The smile, scowl, or grimace evident on your face is reflected in your organs as a change in chemistry. Anyone able to wield a gastroscope, or fibre-optic tube, can observe how the lining of the stomach blanches with stress. Knowing how emotions affect our organs, the expressions 'gut feeling', and 'have a heart', take on a whole new meaning. It also explains how emotions affect our physical health.

The following conditions are related to anxiety and stress: migraine, tension headaches, gastritis, peptic ulcer disease, hypertension, eczema, rosacea, irritable bowel syndrome, muscle tension and insomnia. The strategies we put in place to deal with anxiety – smoking, over- and undereating, overwork, alcohol abuse, prescription and recreational drugs – lead to further physical ailments such as heart attacks, strokes, emphysema, kidney damage, addiction and alcoholism, which result in yet more anxiety. These conditions, in turn, can lead to other difficulties. Being obese makes one susceptible to arthritis and diabetes, with its many complications like blindness, kidney failure and amputation of the legs. Obese people and smokers are far more likely to develop complications should they need an operation.

***

A forty-three-year-old man arrived at the clinic complaining of chest pain that had come on while driving. Although the characteristics of the pain were not typical of heart disease and the ECG was normal, I was concerned. He was hypertensive and a smoker, his cholesterol was high, and he told me that, when he was a boy, his father had died of a heart attack. The pain had only started half an hour previously, so it was too early to do a spot blood check for raised cardiac enzymes. I explained that I wanted to refer him by ambulance to the local hospital, so that a cardiologist could monitor him further in the ICU.

The man sat up and pulled off the oxygen mask. He exclaimed: 'I am not having a heart attack! I have a four-year-old son at home!' Despite my every attempt to dissuade him, he insisted that we take down his drip, and he left.

His fear was so overwhelming it rendered him incapable of reason. His response to his predicament was to insist that it was not happening, and to remove himself from any available help. To understand this, we need to check in with recent discoveries in neuroscience concerning how and why fear operates in the body.

Largely unbeknown to us, we are constantly monitoring our bodies to assess whether all is well, and what needs to be adjusted if there is something amiss. Am I too hot? Too cold? Am I hungry? Am I aroused? If the incoming signals generate a feeling of discomfort, the brainstem issues outgoing signals to the parts of the brain designated to respond to these basic needs by initiating appropriate movement. Take the jacket off, or put it on. Move to a more comfortable spot. Find food, or sex.

We are also continuously surveying our environment. If I see a snake while walking on the mountain, I instinctively freeze. My viscera respond to this sight as well, in preparation to protect myself from possible danger – my heart rate goes up, my breathing gets shallower, and blood shunts from my stomach to my muscles in preparation for flight. Many of these neurological pathways are hard-wired, reflexive, not requiring conscious reflection. When you need to respond to a threat, it would be counter-productive to have to think about it first.

Attaching emotions to experiences is invaluable, as they provide us with a guide to action. Yet emotions, precisely because of instances like those described above, are frequently seen as problematic, unreliable and subjective. Until recently, they were not studied by any self-respecting neuroscientist.

The invention of real-time imaging has allowed scientists better access to subjective experience. The neuroscientist Antonio Damasio, in *The Feeling of What Happens*, says that emotion and reason are no longer presumed to be in opposition. His research shows that our emotions are integral to our decision-making processes, and that the superstructure of reason cannot operate properly without a firm emotional base.[43]

Fear has an essential function that is far more subtle than the crude fight, flight or freeze. Fear can be protective in reminding us of similar situations we have encountered.

Damasio describes a woman who, as a result of a rare disorder, developed deposits of calcium in her amygdale, the seat of the fear response in the brain. This woman was a friendly, compassionate, generous person, and it was easy to like her. Yet she was repeatedly abused in relationships, and was unable to stop repeating her error in trusting untrustworthy people, purely because she was incapable of feeling fear. Her alarm bell – her warning system – was encrusted with calcium.

***

The essence of consciousness is a relationship: I feel like *this* in relationship to *that*. This connection reflects the fact that our needs can only be satisfied by things that exist beyond ourselves.

Damasio describes consciousness as the spontaneous ability of an organism to step back metaphorically and observe life, including him/herself, and to make associations about the observations, stringing them into a non-verbal and repeatable story about what the organism is living through.[44]

Consciousness gives us the ability to sense both the external and the inner worlds in the present, and to correlate the current experience with our past perceptions. For example, when I see and hear and touch and smell an object which I have learnt to recognise as Brother, at the same time, instantaneously, I reconstruct all my feeling associations with this person that were set up long ago.

This is not a simple matter, as there will always be a range of associated feelings. If my experience of Brother has been unhappy, the range evoked might include fear, longing (shown bio-chemically to be associated with loss and panic) and anger. Seeing Brother in real-time, or even being on the receiving end of any behaviour from another person that reminds me of Brother, will evoke these old visceral responses we call emotion. Emotion motivates action; the word itself – e-motion – embodies movement. Unhappy to see Brother, I might scowl, go silent, smile unconvincingly, leave the room, or become belligerent: Freeze, flight or fight.

The symptom of chest pain in my patient triggered the unbearable visceral memory of his father's death when he was a boy, and the fear that he might inflict that same fate on his own child. He had a knee-jerk response to my assessment and to his fears for his son's wellbeing, decided that my concern was misplaced and walked away.

It is possible that his chest pain was not brought on by poor perfusion of his heart muscle. But it is preferable to assess the situation fully before deciding on a course of action. Secondary consciousness comes in here. In humans it is more developed than in most other animals due to the filtering function of the frontal lobes. This brain structure allows for a more differentiated response to a situation, as opposed to a reflexive reaction. We have recognised this for some time – people who have severely damaged frontal lobes have limited capacity for reflection, and can exhibit unmediated, disinhibited and antisocial behaviour.

My patient had never injured his frontal lobes, but in these circumstances, he was not able to employ them effectively. The job of this area of the brain is to insert directed thinking and attention between perception of an event and action. The pause generated allows us to run through possible responses to a situation as well as the probable consequences, and to choose the most appropriate one. In other words, the pause allows us to think. Thinking is imagining.

This ability to review options for action, through the frontal lobe functions of impulse control, assessment, judgement, motivation and modification, is one that needs to be exercised. It can take a lifetime to recognise patterns of reaction that are generated entirely out of our own self-referential story, and not to foist them on others as though they were the truth.

The neuropsychologist Mark Solms[45] points out the irony that the frontal lobes are the seat of free will precisely because of their effect of inhibition on human behaviour. Through impulse control, human beings are freed from stereotypical reactions.

Impulse control is a factor that allows for loving, considerate behaviour. If I am hungry, I can refrain from gobbling all the food so as to share it with others who are also hungry. If I am sexually aroused, I can restrain myself from imposing myself inappropriately on another person. If I am beside myself with anger, I can stop myself from inflicting harm on others.

However, inhibition is not only a helpful attribute. It can also result in repression of aspects of one's core humanity. For example, parental injunctions, based on the social practices of the times, like boys don't cry, or a decent woman wouldn't walk like that, or art is a waste of time, can become word restrictions embedded within neural circuits, playing havoc later with emotional, sexual and creative life.

As we know, emotions too are not always good guides. Sometimes we misread the situation completely, and feel terrible about something that had absolutely nothing to do with us. Someone doesn't greet us in the street, and we take it as a personal affront; meanwhile she hasn't got her contact lenses in. Or the emotion we attached to an event when we were dependent and vulnerable children, might have engendered an action plan appropriate only for that situation. The fear and rage a boy might feel at being bullied at boarding school, where there was no-one to protect him, could result in him dissociating from those feelings as a self-protective strategy. Later, as an independent adult in the workplace and in a marriage, when situations inevitably arise that make him feel threatened, he dissociates, even though the strategy is no longer helpful.

***

Anxiety in infants is mediated by the caregiver. A baby is a totally vulnerable creature, who can complain loudly to draw attention to discomfort and distress, but cannot satisfy any need by herself.

The child psychologist, John Bowlby, states that it is essential for the developing infant to have a secure relationship with adult caregivers for normal social and emotional development to occur. We have evidence through real-time imaging of the brain that the primary caregiver's attitude to life shapes the development of part of the child's brain called the orbito-frontal cortex (OFC), and thereby the way she will experience the world.[46]

The child develops patterns of attachment which lead to what Bowlby calls an internal working model. This guides the individual's feelings, thoughts, and expectations in later relationships. An internal working model might include feeling that you are unwanted, or that people cannot be trusted, that you must always look after number one, or that you are the golden child. These powerful beliefs are handed down from parents to their offspring, even before they learn to speak.

How robustly the OFC develops in early life has enormous consequences. Where physical neglect is extreme, as was documented in some state-run Romanian orphanages towards the end of the twentieth century, there was almost no development or electrical activity found in the OFCs of these young children.

Megan Gunnarv[47] observed that mothers responded differently to their children's distress. Those who had good rapport with their children had little trouble in calming them when they were confronted with a strange situation. In contrast, mothers with insecure attachments had difficulty in reducing the fear in their children. Gunnar says, 'They seemed to think it was their job to change the child, to make the child look bold.' She notes that secure attachments absorb the anxiety from strange or scary events. Without this buffer, children suffer more stress. Gunnar concludes that 'The secure children seemed to be saying, "This is scary but I feel safe."'

***

We can see in animals that have been abused how their fear response has been distorted. A friend took a stray on as company for his dog. It soon became evident that the stray had been viciously and randomly hurt. Whenever there was a loud noise or a sudden movement, the dog would freeze, shaking and trembling, sometimes voiding urine, and on occasion, he would turn on the other dog unprovoked and bite him. Nothing the caring and patient family could do would change his habitual response. His circumstances had changed, but he could only interpret the world in the way he had first experienced it at the time his brain was developing. In response to a perceived threat, all he is able to do is either dissociate or become aggressive himself. The dog is becoming increasingly difficult to live with, and my friend is concerned for his other dog's safety.

People who have been severely traumatised during the first years of life might also behave in extreme and destructive ways. A man in a pub who observes another man looking over at him with a particular expression might punch him. In a similar way that the knee-jerk reflex involves a stimulus followed by an immediate reaction – the leg kicks out – the man in the pub hits out before he stops to consider his perception and his options. Such reflex actions do not allow other information in.

In the knee-jerk this is as it should be; the reflex helps to maintain posture and balance, and allows one to walk without consciously thinking about each step. In the pub scenario, however, the man has his perception of threat hard-wired to memories linked to a habitually aggressive reaction, creating problems for himself and for those around him. If he were able to access the magnificent benefit of the frontal cortex, a network of neurons would be activated where he could reflect on his impressions and assess his options for a nuanced response.

Damasio proposes that consciousness emerges as images rather than words; by images he means patterns established in the brain by any stimulus: emotion, smell, movement, touch, sight. He says, that in any situation, in order for us to choose an appropriate action, we need to be able to refer to a bank of good internal images constellated from previous experiences. We are then able to review a range of images that represent different options, different scenarios, and different outcomes before we act. Good actions, he maintains, need the company of good images.[48]

Recent findings show that the brain remains capable of change throughout a lifetime. It is possible for someone like the man in the pub to release himself from the terrible bind of poor responses and choices. If he makes meaningful human connection with another who has the capacity – unlike his original caregiver – to provide a relationship which acts as a container of care, the neural circuitry in his brain can reset itself by making new connections.

This is the cornerstone of psychotherapy and is present in the mentoring system offered by twelve step programmes like Alcoholics Anonymous.

A premise of this book is that if we are activated by disturbing events, yet manage to resist the knee-jerk response, engaging in creative acts can assist us to imagine and to think in the pause. It can help us to develop our internal images which might release us from the habits that bind us.

***

DAWN GARISCH

11. Not Waving, but Drowning

i'm thinking: my nightmare
smoking, thinking, smoking

what am i going to
do about that, the encroachment
of the neighbour's wall the

inbox choking with e-mails
everywhere the world tilting
towards me the day so i

get up at night, four in the
morning, get it
started so i can push back

Alan Finlay[49]

The Archives of Neurology[50] published a case in 2003 of a man who developed paedophilia at the age of forty. Despite knowing that his obsession was unacceptable, he could not restrain himself from acting on his impulses. This destroyed his marriage and resulted in a prison sentence. Just before going to prison, he developed terrible headaches and went to an emergency room where a tumour of the OFC was discovered and later removed. After surgery, the drive for sexual behaviour towards children disappeared.

This case study of a rare cause of an obsessive-compulsive disorder illustrates both the site and intransigence of defective impulse control. Tension and anxiety builds incrementally until the sufferer acts in order to get relief, even though the consequences of acting might have predictably negative and even disastrous consequences. The sufferer acts, even in the knowledge that the relief will not last, and that the compulsion will repeat itself endlessly. To understand the failure of impulse control in addiction in all its guises – sex, drugs, gambling, alcohol, eating, cutting, smoking, and even shopping – one must recognise that an addict only feels normal for the brief period after he or she has ácted on the compulsion.

The hallmarks of addiction, according to the twelve step programme, are deceit, denial, justification and manipulation. An addict has to have access to a regular fix, and his day is organised around this need, using these four tools to get it.

All these features of addiction are present in our contemporary way of life. Our consumer society has trained us to expect immediate gratification, with credit cards forced on us from every direction, with fast foods available day and night without even having to get out of the car, with instant foods and beverages. Nowadays you can buy an instant lawn, or even an instant bonzai, the very symbol of a slow and patient art.

Most of us have some form of compulsion. We live in an addictive, hyperactive, attention-deficit-disordered and entitled society. We are anxious. We want relief, and we want it now, no matter whether we, or the earth, can afford it. We trade temporary, superficial relief of our immediate suffering for permanent disability and disaster.

Addicts are the very last to know that they have a problem, even as their lives fall apart around them. Denial runs deeply in all of us, yet it seems counter-evolutionary. It seems to fly in the face of the life-force itself, which sends out increasingly urgent distress signals in the form of illness, accidents, pollution, plagues, water and food shortages, extinctions and increasingly violent natural disasters.

In my career as a doctor I have seen many people eat, smoke, drug, drink and stress themselves to death. Contrary to logic and the drive towards life, we are capable of killing ourselves through obsessive-compulsive behaviours, anxiety and denial. The consequences of these human tendencies:

pollution, destruction of ecosystems, over-exploitation of natural resources and overpopulation, may well be fuelling climate change.

That is something to be anxious about.

***

Stress is a normal part of life, part of the call to action and change, but the unrelenting, pervasive nature of stress in the modern world is a serious problem. In physics, stress is the term for a force or system of forces producing deformation or strain. In human life it implies a situation where the individual has to endure something, or is making efforts, beyond the limits of his capacity. Eventually, something has to give.

Many of my patients work too hard and too many hours, whether they are executives or shelf-packers. Often they are doing the work of two people. When ill, many refuse to go off sick; instead they eat a handful of pills and go straight back to the workplace. They don't have time to develop other aspects of their lives, from their relationships to their creative pursuits. They default on exercise and on eating nutritious meals. Some of my patients subsist on fast foods. They get bladder infections because they don't have time to go to the toilet. They take their problems to bed with them, and worry into the night. They do not have time to stop and pay attention to what is happening to them.

When we fail to identify this as abuse, we fail ourselves. Collectively, we do not challenge the way that things have been set up. Human beings created this system, so it is possible for human beings to change it.

Anxiety and stress activate the neural and endocrine pathways that prepare the body to resolve the cause of the problem – flight, fight or play dead. The hypothalamus in the brain, working via the pituitary gland and the sympathetic nervous system, stimulates the adrenal glands to release adrenalin, noradrenalin and corticosteroids. These are called either hormones or neurotransmitters, depending on where they are found in the body, but in 1984 the neuroscientist Francis Schmitt suggested that the whole gamut of these agents should instead be called information substances.[51] Dozens have been identified that are associated with our emotions and the physiological changes that accompany them.

The information molecules released by fear and stress, heart rate, blood pressure and blood glucose. They divert blood away from the digestive tract and towards the brain and skeletal muscles. Emotionally, we might experience this as a pounding heart, sweaty palms, tense muscles and butterflies in the stomach. We become primed for action to resolve the situation, and to release and move on from this physiological state. In the modern world with its pervasive and layered stressors, the cause of the stress is not so easily dispatched. It is like being all dressed up with nowhere to go, and we end up chronically stimulated for a response that is curtailed.

Persistent stress causes a protracted increase in the information molecules released to resolve the situation. Chronic exposure to these agents results in a decreased sensitivity at the receptor sites, which causes more to be released, with a subsequent build-up of the molecules.

Dr Candace Pert proposes that this situation results in a disruption of the normal fluctuations of other hormones and neurotransmitters in the body;[52] consequently the flow of information, processes and emotion necessary for optimal health are jeopardised. We become sick. We lose concentration and have an accident. The body trips us up, asking us to reconsider.

***

DAWN GARISCH

12. Denial, Deception and Illusion

on the frontlines the mirror the paper the morning
news closely shaves off the edges of the real
world

Kai Lossgott[53]

A patient came to see me because she had lost her temper at work and had walked out. She was very upset with herself as she had never done this before.

She identified herself as someone who is good at helping others. She works long hours, often with unpaid overtime, for a demanding employer who hardly ever takes leave herself. This woman is the kind of person who has extreme difficulty saying no to anyone else, although she says no to herself and her body all the time – a body that is increasingly overweight, exhausted and in pain.

Interestingly, she is also unconsciously saying no to her daughter, to whom she does not pay much attention because her job takes up so much space and time. The daughter is exhibiting distress signals too, under-achieving at school and overeating.

On taking a medical history, I discovered that this woman has atrial fibrillation, a condition where the entry chambers of the heart do not contract properly, sending irregular impulses to the ventricles, which in turn cause an irregular heart beat and pulse. This condition is associated with an excess of stress, alcohol, nicotine- and caffeine-containing substances like tea, coffee, colas and some medications. If the normal rhythm of the atria cannot be restored by addressing these aggravating factors, or through medication or electric shock therapy to the heart, then blood clots can form in the atria due to the turbulent blood flow. These can break away and become lodged in the brain, depriving neural tissue of oxygen and causing a stroke, resulting in disability or death. It is therefore essential for such patients to take a blood-thinning medication called coumadin.

Taking coumadin itself can be hazardous: if you take too much, you can haemorrhage, and if you take too little it won't be effective. To ensure that the patient is taking the correct dose, her blood must be tested every three to four weeks. Even though this patient knew why it was essential to have her blood checked, she told me she had been too busy to do so for over six months.

Many physical difficulties we see in the consulting rooms are self-inflicted. People usually have the means to keep themselves healthy and to help themselves to heal, yet curiously we often choose lifestyles that run counter to health and healing, and which make enormous demands on the restorative capabilities of the body.

A doctor is a consultant in the field of health and healing, and must advise a client concerning matters of wellbeing. This includes trying to help a patient break through self-deception. Most of the time this is an unbelievably difficult and dispiriting task. Many people persist with denial even in the face of crippling illness. As an intern I was impressed by the attitude of an obese woman who was admitted for a diabetic complication. After receiving life-saving and costly interventions, her blood sugar was restored to normal. As I was doing the paperwork at her bedside to discharge her, she admitted that she could not wait to get home for a lovely white bread sandwich with peanut butter and syrup.

On another occasion I was on duty in the obstetric ward when the flying squad arrived, sirens blaring. They brought in a large woman who had started haemorrhaging six months into her pregnancy. This can happen if the placenta starts to come away from the uterine wall. The likelihood of losing the baby in this situation is high. It was her first pregnancy, and she was understandably distressed. She said she could no longer feel foetal movements. The drip was up and running, and we immediately sent blood off for cross-matching. When we could not find a foetal heartbeat on the monitor, we feared the worst. But the ultrasound showed no pregnancy. The woman was having a normal period. In her desire for a child, she had stopped menstruating for six months, had put on weight, and had felt foetal movements.

As a doctor I deal with denial every day, and I need to understand it better. As a writer, it is a fascinating aspect of the human condition. And as a human being, I have had to face my own capacity for not seeing things that were staring me in the face.

Denial prevents us from having the insights necessary to fuel appropriate action, such as acknowledging evidence that a revered leader has turned out not to be an honourable man and is instead a poor role model, or that a loaf in the supermarket labelled 'health bread' contains artificial ingredients and has a token coating of whole wheat.

***

My in-tray today contained a glossy pamphlet advertising a conference for medical professionals entitled 'Medical Aesthetics'. On the cover was a soft-porn shot of the face of a young blonde model picked for her child-like features. Her full and perfect lips were suggestively parted. Held vertically up to her mouth, the tip of a needle attached to a syringe was about to penetrate her lacquered upper lip. The subliminal associations were: oral sex, paedophilia, abuse, addiction, and fixing something that is not broken.

Which is about right. The underbelly of plastic surgery is about retaining the illusion of youth, sexual appeal and availability through abusive and addictive attitudes to the body, which is deemed never good enough.

This meeting is not a couple of hours after work. It is a four-day extravaganza, with four international speakers and a long line-up of local practitioners. Topics include:

- Treatments to improve the external genitalia's aesthetic appearance
- The difficult lip
- Non-surgical options for nose reshaping and African nose treatments
- Peels and other resurfacings
- Rejuvenating neglected areas
- Home devices
- The ageing athlete
- The exploding male aesthetic market

We all have something about our bodies that we do not like. Whatever it is, if you have the money, you will be able to find a doctor who will be prepared to alter it for you.

As I am growing older, my body is changing. It comes as a shock to see evidence of the passing of time etched into my own tissues. And it appears to have arrived overnight. I glance at my thighs and notice small red veins sprouting under my skin. In the mirror I see sags around my eyes, and a slackening around my jaw.

My first impulse is surgery. Cut it off, take it out, laser it away, whatever. Restore me to myself, whatever that is.

I rein myself in, caught between the shame of ageing and the shame of feeling ashamed of ageing. I decide that I will only go for plastic surgery when I am completely comfortable with the way my body is as she grows older. Of course, when I am comfortable with how I look there is no way I will let anyone near my face with a knife.

I have a sense that, when we side with an idea of perfection and try to rid ourselves of everything that hints at imperfection, we become increasingly lopsided, alienated from the totality of who we are. As a writer, I know how much character matters. The idiosyncrasies of my physical shape and facial contour are important to who I am. These attributes are accentuated and given more definition by time.

An hypothesis: Coming to terms with my face is coming to terms with my life.

***

Professor Loyal Rue in his book *By The Grace of Guile* points out that our understanding of ourselves and of the world is a construct based on perception, and the meaning we attach to that which we perceive. We are perpetually flooded with information about our inner state and that of the exterior world, and often the information is in conflict.

It is the role of the frontal lobes to sort and organise data into some kind of congruence. That congruence is the foundation from which we make the necessary judgements to plan and execute a course of action. Judgement implies that we are able to check our perceptions against the truth – something that we are sometimes woefully incapable of, or unwilling to do.

In denial, we either make no attempt to check whether an assumption is true, or we actively make attempts to bolster a skewed idea of reality. A friend, having warned her drug-abusing son that her home is a drug-free zone, made her son and his friend strip down to their underpants on their return late one night. She found marijuana hidden in their socks, and called the other boy's mother to come and fetch her son. When the mother arrived, she was furious about my friend's assertion. She turned to her son, declaring, 'You didn't have drugs on you, did you?' Her son was only too pleased to comply with his mother's demand that he deny it.

Rue postulates that there are three motive forces in the human psyche, curiosity, hedonism and self-esteem, and it is often the conflict between these areas that force us to choose between satisfying one while denying another. In the drug-denying story, the friend's mother's self-esteem was at stake, so she wasn't about to become curious about her son's habits.

Denial is a psychological device whereby painful truths are not admitted. We refuse to acknowledge what is right in front of us, even when it is apparent to everyone else, for example, that one is an alcoholic. A friend from a twelve step programme says denial is wonderful while it is operating, because it allows you to think that everything is fine in circumstances that might otherwise be untenable, like not knowing that your spouse is cheating on you, or believing that your adolescent son's large crop of plants behind the garage, that he harvests and sells, indicates an interest in horticulture.

In order to deceive ourselves, we must be capable of accepting as truth one set of perceptions and cancelling out any contradictory information. Rue suggests that this capacity to pull the wool over our own eyes helps individuals, relationships and groupings to cohere and function altruistically as though inherent contradictions were not present. He says it allows us to subscribe to the ideas of marriage, a rainbow nation, and even the stock exchange.

James Hollis[54] warns against the religious, political and psychological constructs in society that encourage us to deny shadow material rather than to engage with the subterranean features of our humanity. He argues that it is the artists and depth psychologists who venture into this difficult terrain, and who are therefore instructive guides in our efforts to heal ourselves and our relationships to others and the earth.

***

Imagine reality.

I love this bumper-sticker advice. Yet our brains hide from our consciousness the fact that we are hiding something. What entity decides what to hide and what to reveal? There is a sorting going on.

We have to cross a threshold to perceive something that we have not been able to notice before. One way is by waiting until we are smacked in the face by the cold fish of reality: when you come home earlier than usual one day to find your husband in bed with your best friend, or when the police come over to question you about your nice, quiet neighbour who has body parts in his fridge. Or you find that the weight you have been gaining constantly for some months despite dieting, followed by cramps that you assume to be a touch of gastro, results astonishingly in a little head popping out between your legs.

Another way to survey for what is really going on – if we don't want to wait for the cold fish – is to do a reality check. Ask everyone around you what they think about the matter under question. If the consensus is that you are too old or drunk to be behind the wheel and are a menace on the road, even if you are of the opinion that your driving is fine and everyone else drives recklessly, perhaps it is time to take note.

Most of us most of the time are very defensive. We discourage feedback. Our self-esteem has been too damaged, or we have been too manipulated by those close to us to be able to take a step back and review the situation. Yet feedback can be lifeblood. We know who we are and, simultaneously, we cannot see ourselves. Literally. Even in the mirror, what we see is a reverse image. We get a surprise when we hear a recording of our own voice.

I find it very discomforting to realise that most people will not say to your face the very thing everyone is discussing about you behind your back. You might consider yourself a kind, caring and devoted doctor, and on the whole you could well be, but, unbeknown to you, your nickname at the referral hospital due to your tendency to refer patients very late, is Dr Death. You might announce that your daughter is an uncaring parasite, but behind your back people might be shaking their heads over what an impossible mother you are.

Moving people over the threshold and out of denial is something I regularly try out in the consulting room. Increasingly, I also attempt to review my own life: a more difficult task than one might imagine. Who can you trust to tell you the truth? What is reality? Is reality a reliable measure of the truth? How important is it to get at the truth?

We have all experienced moments where the world or life turns out to be different from what we thought it was. The terrible moment you break through denial and discover that your daughter is a heroin addict, that your heart or lungs have been irreversibly damaged due to poor lifestyle choices, that your government has reneged on its promises, that the lump in your breast that you have been hoping will go away by itself is cancer, that your doctor, homeopath or energy healer cannot prevent you from dying, that AIDS is caused by a virus, that having sex without contraceptive protection has resulted in a pregnancy.

We have all at some point been forced to change the way we see things.

***

Every day I meet people who take medication for high blood pressure, high cholesterol levels, diabetes and joint pain rather than change what they eat and lose weight, who take antidepressants and anxiolytics rather than leave a chronically abusive job or marriage, or take asthma medication rather than stop smoking or find a new home for the cats. Athletes arrive regularly at the clinic for injections of anti-inflammatories so that they can carry on running. They want the doctor to collude with the abuser.

We all have our blind spots. Some seem more mind-boggling than others, especially when they are not yours. The pharmaceutical companies know there is a fortune to be made out of this human tendency to be blind to the thing that is in front of you. There is even a glossy advertisement that promotes an antacid as treatment for our modern lifestyle. The visual depicts cigarettes, alcohol, caffeine, fast food and stress – all of which promote indigestion. The explicit message is: you don't have to change your ways, just pop one of our products.

A sales representative for anti-inflammatories predicted with a gleam in his eye that arthritis is going to increase enormously in the upcoming generation due to the amount of time growing children spend in front of the television and the computer instead of running around with a ball, climbing a tree or dancing. Strenuous movement is necessary to develop normal joints.

I sometimes ask patients what they do for exercise, and a surprising number tell me that they walk around at work.

A patient of mine who had an ongoing battle with her weight, lost two kilograms in a week. She rewarded herself by going out and ordering a piece of cake. This woman has an eating disorder, which is a form of addiction. Addiction, says the twelve step programme, is a disorder of thinking. But addictive thinking is not confined to addicts. We all rationalise, justify, manipulate, deny and lie to ourselves about the bad habits we are terrified to give up.

It seems that we cannot rely on logic alone to release us. We need a little help from non-rational quarters.

***

13. Physician, Heal Thyself

Home
bit my hand last night;
the door released me from its jaw
then skulked away, leaving me
to dance upon a bright hot
coin of pain.[55]

Again I am learning something I thought I knew, but did not really understand: I cannot write this book from the outside. I cannot write it retrospectively, from a superior vantage point, casting a wise eye back into the ignorant past. I, too, am deep in the soup, clinging to a noodle.

This book has to be written from the inside, from the here and now, out of current trial and error, out of the pain, confusion and relief of the present. By the act of taking up my pen to put down all that I have discovered as a doctor and a scribe, I have awoken ancient ghosts and poets. They seethe eagerly at my elbow, seeking to influence my life through my writing, and my writing through my life.

For the past few months I have had pain in my upper and lower teeth on the left. My dentist tried this and that, but could not diagnose the cause. I have been chewing on the right side only, and I dread the pain of the cold rinse after brushing. I am raging about the terrible dentist who ruined my teeth when I was a child. He was a character out of a horror movie, surly, sadistic, and a hater of children.

My current dentist, a sweet, concerned man and a pianist, asks me: 'Do you grind your teeth at night?' Of course not. It is a question I have asked my patients often enough when trying to diagnose unusual cases of headache or earache. It might apply to a patient, but not to me. I am not that neurotic, and I am not stressed. 'You have well developed masseter muscles,' he persists, irritatingly. 'Do you clench your teeth at night?'

Never.

Ever since he dangled this question, I have been aware, subliminally, that I clench my teeth when I swallow or turn while sleeping.

I am shocked. I know about the unconscious, yet when I stumble upon certain manifestations of it in my own life, I can hardly believe it. How could I have been unaware for all these years that I clench my teeth at night? How long has this been going on behind my back? Long enough to cause dental pulp to go into revolt, screaming. Now I must wear a bite plate at night, like a bit inserted to tame the nocturnal spirit that seizes me.

The bite plate is slowly reducing my symptoms, but I cannot stop at that. What comes to mind is wailing and gnashing of teeth. I have always understood this phrase as synonymous with grief, but googling it, I discover that it has more to do with rage, anguish and hatred. Yes, I do experience these feelings. On and off during my life I have bitten my nails while reading ever since I went to boarding school at the age of nine. Annoying. Intractable, even though I have bought gloves (which I never wear) and consider sitting on my hands while engrossed in a book.

Also, I sucked my thumb until the age of six. There is a mouth thing going on.

⁎⁎

In a dream last night, my son, suddenly back to age nine, kissed the President of Argentina, a woman who, in my dream, is married to the King of Naples. The kiss was indifferent, dutiful; they were merely going through the motions. It was a pretence, underneath which lay their teeth – rage and aggression. A kiss can become a bite in a nanosecond.

These images of mouths and teeth, hunger and rage are sunk deep into my flesh – my muscles are tense and inflamed, in pain and crackling with crepitus. Now that the tension and pain of my autoimmune and psychological condition has entered my jaw, expanding, amplifying my process and drawing more attention to itself, again I feel despair. My body has lived in varying degrees of pain for so long, I am desperately sorry for her. Like a slave or a child, she is forced to bear the unbearable, and I don't know how to help her.

Yes, I have worked with my body processes most of my life, through therapy, dance, embodied imagination, process work, reiki, family constellation therapy and Tomatis, and I have learnt a huge amount about myself and the world, all of which has helped me with this difficult and beautiful gift of life, all of which I am grateful for. Yes, I have come to a place where I think I have let go of cure, and accepted that there are limits to being human, starting with death, and that I live with an incurable, chronic illness. Yes, this illness has led me by the nose down alleys I would never have gone down otherwise. It has made me a better doctor, a better person. It has released more compassion in me, and has opened my mind and my physical self to the complexity of illness and health and what it is to be human.

This dreadful ancestral curse I carry, handed down in my genes – HLA B27 – has also been a blessing. But I am tired of pain. I weep for the suffering of my body, a body that has served me so well. The unconscious still rides her, still has her muscles in its bony grip. I want to rage: what else do you want of me? Why won't you speak to me?

For the moment, my body stays mute.

***

Doctors are in trouble. They have a higher than average incidence of suicide, addiction and depression. At a recent lecture for doctors on workaholism, the lecturer pointed out that we are amongst the worst. Medical students are selected for it. Their high school grades largely determine whether they will be accepted into medical school. The teenagers entering the halls of learning for the medical profession have already proven themselves to be both driven and high achievers, attributes that do not come with rebelliousness. Doctors are therefore more likely to accept abusive working conditions. During my neurosurgery internship I was expected to work a one-hundred-and-ten-hour week. They are also less likely than the general population to protest, or to go on strike.

Doctors do complain, however – amongst themselves. It is rare to go to a doctors' meeting without being snagged by a colleague grumbling about income, medical aids or the impending Health Insurance Act.

It's enough to make anyone clench their teeth.

***

Today I visited the Tibetan Tea House to witness some visiting Buddhist monks creating a sand mandala. They do this as their life work, spending days or even weeks making exquisitely intricate and symmetrical patterns within a large circle using naturally coloured sand. Just watching them work gave me backache; it also moved me to the brink of tears. When they have finished, they equally gently and carefully sweep their creation up, section by section. They then carry the sand to a body of water nearby, and deposit it into the flow. It is a symbolic act of distributing harmony and beauty via the rivers and oceans to the world.

Years ago, when I was first told about this practice, I remember feeling puzzled, even disdainful. Something in my chest hurt at the thought of painstaking work coming to nothing, and beauty deliberately being destroyed. Only now that I am in the second half of life have I begun to understand the value of such an act. All the beautiful constructs we work hard to put in place during the first part of our lives – relationships, children, financial security, a home, a career, works of art – will be swept away at death. We might leave children behind when we die, or paintings, or possessions and money, but our bodies will decay back into the land. Our children's bodies will follow, as well as the musical scores and mosaics and literature and bank notes; everything eventually will be reclaimed, will disintegrate and dissolve.

The study of death at medical school was confined to the anatomy laboratory, the post-mortem room and the forensic mortuary, which were simultaneously macabre and academic. The practice of medicine had to do with the living. It was about living. Our long training was designed to defeat illness and prolong life. Implicitly, for most doctors, death is an adversary.

When my own father developed an illness which paralysed him slowly over many months, a senior neurologist investigated him thoroughly, but could not find a cause. My father deteriorated until he was unable to walk, feed himself, or look after himself in any way. He lost an enormous amount of weight, and was struggling to come to terms with his terrible disability.

To my distress, the neurologist suggested yet another battery of tests. I approached this respected man who had taught me previously, and asked him whether it would not be better to stop investigating my father and help him prepare for death. 'You must *never* give up,' he reprimanded, in a tone that conveyed I had uttered a blasphemy.

The first two occasions when people died in my care during my internship I felt devastated. There was no-one to talk to about it, no mentoring, no debriefing. I felt overwhelmed and very alone.

Late one night, an elderly man who was having a heart attack was admitted to my ward. I called the cardiology registrar, who refused him admission to ICU because of his age, as was the state hospital policy. He told me to administer morphine, then left me at the bedside. The curtains around the bed were drawn and the bedside light was on. The dying stranger and I were brought together by this moment, illuminated in the same pool of light in an otherwise darkened ward in the middle of the night. He wasn't coping with the tremendous crushing pain in his chest; sweat was trickling down his temples. He kept begging me to help him. In the absence of any other options, I kept on giving him intravenous morphine until his eyes emptied and he stopped breathing. His coronary thrombosis probably killed him, but I was left worrying that I had done so with a morphine overdose. Six years in medical school had not prepared me for this. I was way out of my depth.

The second occasion involved a middle-aged woman who had recently been operated on for a subdural haematoma - a collection of blood that slowly accumulates under the skull after trauma, compressing the brain. The neurosurgeons had cut her scalp open, then had drilled burr holes into the skull to drain the blood. Then she had been sent to a convalescent hospital to recover.

One morning she was discovered semi-conscious. The doctor in charge was concerned that the blood was re-accumulating, and had booked her for transfer back to our hospital for urgent scanning and probable surgery. It took the whole day for her to be transferred, and by the time she arrived in the neurosurgery ward, she was in a coma. The CT scanner was occupied with another patient, and the neurosurgery registrar was in theatre. Soon after arriving, she stopped breathing.

I rang the bell for help, and the cardiology registrar arrived with the resuscitation equipment and put the patient on a ventilator. Her heart was still going, but she was deeply unconscious. I called the neurosurgery registrar in theatre on the intercom. He said her only chance was for someone to stick a brain needle in through the burr hole in her skull and extract the blood. The cardiology registrar threw up his hands, saying it was not part of his job description, so I found myself, three months into my apprenticeship, trying to perform brain surgery in the middle of a ward on a dying patient. All I managed to suck out of her head was brain tissue; then she died.

This happened during my two-month stint on the neurosurgery ward where interns were expected to work every day and every second night. Why the senior staff allowed this state of affairs – which amounts to malpractice – I do not know. I was too afraid, exhausted and powerless to speak out. Abusing the junior members of staff meant that the patients received sub-standard care. The system also seemed designed to make us numb.

While still a student, my tutorial group arrived for a clinical session in the surgical ward. The surgeon took us to stand at a bed around which the curtains had been drawn. Lying before us was an unconscious man who was barely alive. The surgeon threw back the bedclothes and pulled up the man's hospital gown. His legs were a deep mottled blue, his penis shrivelled, his chest sucking in air sporadically.

The surgeon proceeded to give us a tutorial around the bed about emboli: blood clots or pieces of plaque that can break off and then lodge in an artery downstream. When blood supply to a limb has been occluded in this manner and the patient is not operated on within six hours, the tissues below the occlusion die off due to lack of oxygen. When muscle tissue dies, it releases myoglobin, a muscle protein. If a large amount of myoglobin is released, it clogs up the kidneys, and the patient goes into renal failure.

This had happened to the patient in front of us. Ischaemia is extremely painful, so it is doubtful that anyone suffering this condition would delay seeking help. The delay lay with the referring doctor, and the surgeon was correctly furious, but the way he expressed his anger was appalling. We stood around this dying man while the surgeon lectured us over his naked body.

***

Recently, I attended my twenty-fifth medical class graduation reunion, a three-day affair. I had kept in touch with only one person from my class of almost two hundred doctors in the intervening years, and she had been a friend since high school. After graduating, I applied for a non-governmental organisation job in industrial health, working with trade unions. There my colleagues were mainly sociologists, industrial hygienists and educators. The people I was working for were largely well, and trying to negotiate for a healthier and safer workplace.

At the time I thought I was working in this area because I believed in socialist principles. It was only at the reunion that I was able to acknowledge that I had been so traumatised by my training in the wards as a medical student and intern that I had run away from both doctors and hospitals.

I could not acknowledge it back then, but I disliked doctors, and I was appalled by a system where I could find myself feeling relief when a patient died en route to the intake ward. Then there would be less work for me to do at three in the morning, and I might be able to snatch a wink of sleep before another full day at work.

***

I am a doctor by default, passively following my sister into medicine because my family decided that it was the best thing for me to do. I do not regret this. It is a real job, where there is plenty of opportunity to make interventions that help others. It is also a privilege, in that you are invited into the lives of strangers to hear their stories. Medicine has also allowed me an economic freedom that many do not have. I have worked part-time for twenty-five years, giving me the space to bring up my children and to pursue my passion.

My first love was always the written word. Books opened their arms to me, offering me a haven, a place to discover a new way of thinking and being. At a young age I got hold of novels that my parents tried to hide from me, like *The Old Man and The Sea*, and stumbled upon authors at the library such as Krishnamurti, and realised that not everyone construed the world the way my parents did. Later I read *Nexus* and understood that, to be a good writer, one has to be able to write from the position of the anti-hero. On reading the Martha Quest novels I woke up to my own body through Doris Lessing's powerful writing.

I wanted to be close to books, to the smell of libraries, with their rows of closed stories waiting with folded arms for me to reach out and take a volume, and open it, and thereby open myself.

If I had had the courage of my passion, I might have become a librarian or a copywriter when I left school. I am so pleased that life had other plans for me. Through doing medicine, I have had to work hard with this split between art and science. I have had to heal myself.

Becoming a doctor prepared me to write this book.

***

Interlude

Mankind owns four things
that are no good at sea –
rudder, anchor, oars,
and the fear of going down.

Antonio Machado[55]

The following is a piece written in 2004 largely from emails I sent friends while on board a ship, and later tacked together. I include it as an example of how identifying and exploring images in both my life and my writing have helped contain my anxiety and distress during times of crisis in health and relationship.

14. Travels in the Eloquent Body

Fire and Ice[57]
27 February

I have woken to a dream: I find myself surprisingly aboard a ship that life has offered, extracting me from my busy land-locked round and thrusting me upon adventure. Five days ago a corporate stranger phoned to say that their ship's doctor had failed his medical; would I like to take his place and go to Antarctica?

Which proves you must be careful what you wish for. For some time I had felt an urgent need to step back from the cauldron of the past four years, hoping that distance and changed surroundings would help to put into perspective the burning pottage of my life.

So here I am, two days out and sailing towards the southern ice, two days out upon a tiny cradle rocked upon the shifting lap of sea. The sea is bigger than your boat, my tenant pointed out the night before I left – and so it is! Expanse is not a big enough word for such a place. Our ship, the *SA Agulhas*, represented by a lump of Prestik on the framed map in the corridor outside the bar, moves daily out upon the blue and away from Cape Town through the grid of latitude and longitude. On deck, where I have spent most of my time thus far, I note the ocean is becoming darker and the air colder with the hint of going somewhere.

DAWN GARISCH

It is thirty-seven years since I was last on board a ship, yet aspects are familiar: long passageways, coils of thick rope, latched metal doors to keep the sea water out. The smells I also recognise, although this is an old research vessel and the odours are distinctly worse. My shower drain is so offensive I am forced to complain repeatedly to the purser, thus establishing my character early on. The bosun's mate employs chemicals and irrigation to no effect. This olfactory assault together with the rolling motion breaks my determination not to get seasick. The bosun assures me worse is to come, so abandoning the floundering theory of mind over matter, I have resorted to medication while my lurching belly learns to travel with the lift and surge.

Therefore, thanks to a miracle of modern medicine, I am at last able to focus and honour my personal roles as scribe and explorer on this expedition, as well as perform my public function as ship's doctor, without a sweaty queasiness gnawing at my acumen. Also, the Captain has agreed to my changing cabins.

Our main mission is to fetch eighteen Germans from the southern ice. Amongst them, I am relieved to hear, is another doctor, a colleague should anything go horribly wrong.

***

My duties: the hospital must be opened for half an hour twice a day; thus far for the remedy of minor ailments. Third mate is my assistant; however when I diagnose gastritis in a nauseous member of the crew, I later discover he has slipped the patient Avomine. This is his domain, and he knows better than the doctor that even sailors can get seasick.

I note with alarm an anaesthetic machine in one corner of the consulting room, and announce loudly that I am no anaesthetist and that any surgery will be performed under local anaesthetic, hoping to discourage anyone from festering their appendix on the side or chopping off an arm. The hospital is well equipped and stocked, with one surprising exception: there are no morning-after pills. Stories have already reached my ears of voyages where students, researchers and officers party on duty-free alcohol, having cast off the mooring ropes of their land lives and their wives. There are only three women aboard out of fifty-three, and pheromones have begun to seep into the air.

No routine for me except for the hospital duties and mealtimes, the latter announced through loudspeakers by a gong housed on the bridge. We hurry to the dining room where good food provides variety otherwise lacking in our seafaring lives, and where company is assured. We sit at tables and see-saw to varying degrees in varying seas, on chairs chained to the floor as warning of times to come. The researchers sit around one table, the officers around another. The rest of the crew are never seen to eat.

It is at these banquets that I get to know my companions: the young weatherman who is getting divorced but wants marriage; the professor of meteorology who has a respectful working relationship with the Rain Queen of Venda; the security officer who flies all over the world trying to stay one step ahead of terrorists and who blows up the sea bed to harvest fish for the barbeque; the ex-sea captain now manager of the shipping company who has only been hijacked on land, never at sea; the head of the scientific team, an oceanographer who has watched *Bridget Jones's Diary* twenty times and finds it hard to delegate, joking her resentment away; a marine biologist who is politically correct and exudes entitlement; a French oceanographer who keeps throwing hugely expensive equipment overboard to study whether climate change is a problem or not; the technical support man who tinkers endlessly in his lab and is supplied by a government research agency that also recommends fishing quotas so that we preserve life in our waters, and whose boss has just been fired but not jailed for poaching massive quantities of abalone; and the government official in charge of overseeing the South African interests in the southern seas who lost his eye to cancer last year and wears an eye patch and, sometimes, a toy parrot pinned to his shoulder.

It is fabulous being the ship's doctor; everyone is nice to me in case they fall under my knife.

***

What I have learnt thus far:

- Antarctica is a huge continent: one and a half times the size of the USA.

- There are sections of sea where water systems collide, causing turbulence, which increases food supply and therefore bird life. We have crossed bands of the ocean alive with birds, and bands where there are none.

- Albatross, that sometimes tail the ship, have a tendon that goes through a hole in a shoulder bone, locking the wing into position. They can therefore glide up to eight thousand kilometres at a time, expending minimal energy by keeping low and using the up-draught over each wave. They go to land to lay eggs and hatch chicks, then leave their chicks a week at a time in order to find food. Their navigational skills are so accurate they can fly straight to a favourite food spot in the ocean two thousand kilometres away.

- I have been advised to stick my laptop to the desk with Prestik, which will prevent it flying across the cabin when we reach the roaring forties.

- The scientists keep dropping things overboard that cost over three million rand in total. The French scientist threw some equipment overboard yesterday that he wasn't supposed to. Last trip the weatherman nearly threw himself overboard with his equipment, as the rope attached to the equipment was also wound around his leg. He tells me in this water you only last fifteen minutes. Even if someone notices you are gone, it takes the ship twenty minutes to turn around. I have to add that it is very hard to fall overboard unless you are a scientist.

***

Having an adventure by oneself has a lot to recommend it. I can invent myself and my day as I please within the margins of the ship. After breakfast and the half hour hospital slot, I lock up and stand a moment, deciding what to do. Join those who are lolling in the weak sun upon the helideck or those watching videos in the lounge, or climb up to the bridge for a chat with one of the mates. First mate is a woman, married to fourth mate, and in charge of cargo and ballast, both of which require complicated management and foresight. Or I can retire to my cabin to tuck myself into my desk where waits my laptop, ready for the next chapter. Or read, or sleep.

Or exercise. This is important as we tend to eat too much. There are two options: a stuffy cabin with artificial light and ventilation crammed with exercise bicycles and rowing machines where you can indulge in the fantasy that you are making a small contribution to the progress of the ship, or a walk around the helipad. I prefer the latter, taking a morning and afternoon constitutional. It is meditational, almost mesmeric. You begin to appreciate the attractiveness of the hamster wheel. One obese colleague noted that if you time it right, you can permanently walk downhill. It is exhilarating to be out in the open with surge of wind and water, and sea birds following in the slipstream.

The bar in the evenings, after a couple of rounds, is rich ground for research. The oceanographer, who cannot abide nudity (why would anyone want to look at *that*), is firing off sexual innuendos after another day of shooting contraptions into the sea. The men respond variously: the meteorologist puts on boeremusiek and offers to dance with her, the Frenchman gets all guttural and starts making porn video clips with his digital camera using close-ups of his fingers, the technician snuffles off to the lab, the security officer asks her if she frequents certain clubs in Bellville, the marine biologist, who has decided he doesn't want to be one, rereads emails from his girlfriend and the ex-sea captain reminisces loudly about his bachelor days in port.

The weatherman takes me on a tour of his duties. Every three hours he must venture outside in all conditions to record wind speed and direction, cloud formation and wave height, humidity, temperature and precipitation. These observations are relayed from his lab to Pretoria where they serve as some of the ingredients that go into the flopped cake presented on the news each night as the weather forecast. While the computer printer chews through endless numbers, he explains to me that his marriage was a waste of time because it had ended, and that he has moved back in with his parents because he cannot bear to go home to an empty flat. He also cannot face what he must now endure in order to find another mate: clubbing, partying, deodorant and regular brushing of his teeth. I suggest that life might have other plans for him, at the same time noting how the weather outside, translated into the movement of the ship, is suddenly exceeding his latest measurements.

***

A storm is upon us, and I must learn how to trust my feet upon unstable ground; should I knock myself out the ship is lost, for I'm the doctor, employed to keep the crew and passengers alive and well. I therefore concentrate on my next step upon the deck, which shifts from ponderous incline to a weightless falling away.

The ocean's presence requires a certain kind of vigilance, encouraging me to leave land thoughts behind and to concentrate on my recovery; I am convalescing from a long internal illness on discovering I was not to get what I thought I wanted, as my marriage too had ended. Life has prescribed an ancient cure: a long voyage out, regular doses of vigorous sea air, cradled sleep and lots of it, good food prepared by other hands, the gentle massage of all my organs by the constant motion of the ship, and interesting company with stories varied, intimate and impersonal as happens when people are thrown together on the anonymity of an island experience, and they can make up who they are as they go along.

Two years out upon my new uncertain map, I'm sailing away from the land of marriage towards areas marked only as places where the dragons live. Two years out and I'm turning around, starting to face forwards to see what lies ahead, what other plans life has for me. My body is relaxing, my vision clearing, and I feel my love of life alive again. I stand on deck and breathe the spindrift wind that sings strange songs about the ship, and watch the solid rolls of water that wake within the ocean's centre gathering themselves into long, confident gestures until they lay themselves to rest upon some distant shore.

***

I am on the bridge watching the lift and slice of our ship's progress through the corrugated seascape when my core flushes with the memory of my first dream, my very first, that arrived when I was four or five. I was at the North Pole, North because there were polar bears around. All about was ice and snow, and I saw with wonder – my first experience of awe – that a fire burnt upon the ice. The ice did not melt, and the fire did not go out. These extremes existed together without destroying each other.

I want to tell the Captain: we are going the wrong way.

3 March

Yesterday we sailed into snow on and off, and now the swell is large enough to lift the propeller regularly out of the water, eliciting a low grumbling growl throughout the ship. We are halfway there, sailing down the Greenwich meridian towards the ice shelf near Neumeyer, the German base. The trip there will be further than the trip back, to accommodate the scientists' needs, and slower because we are sailing into wind and swell. Daily we get satellite information about the sea ice which drifts and breaks and packs constantly around Antarctica. The *SA Agulhas's* bow is ice strengthened, so when we arrive at the frozen sea, the ship can ride up onto it, the weight of the vessel breaking through ice up to seventy centimetres deep.

We saw our first ice floe today. The Captain tells me icebergs form from glaciers and ice floes break off from the ice shelf – that skirt of ice sliding slowly off the continent of Antarctica. Last year an ice floe the size of Ireland broke off, causing havoc with weather patterns. The biggest one the Captain has seen, at night on radar, was twenty-five kilometres long. An iceberg can be the size of an ocean liner above water, but the dangerous ones, called growlers, are no bigger than a piano but can sink a ship. These are often black due to being made of old compressed ice, hardly project above water and are detected with difficulty at night despite using radar and infrared binoculars. The atmosphere on the bridge is tense in these waters.

Antarctica is a mountainous continent; the highest peak, the Vinson Massif, is over five thousand meters above sea level. I have learnt too that the South Pole is actually nine meters below sea level, but the ice above it is nearly three kilometres thick; newcomers to the area have to deal with both the cold and with altitude sickness. It is also very dry as any humidity precipitates as snow.

***

A disappointment: the Germans who have chartered the ship at R100 000 a day to fetch them from the ice, have ordered that no-one is to leave the ship when we arrive at the shelf. They worry that we might be in the way and take up precious time, or that we might wander off and fall into a crevasse. It will take them two days to load their cores of ice, also their waste, as according to the Antarctic Treaty nothing may remain behind.

So I am reminded that it's the journey that's important, not the destination. Each day I spend time contemplating the waves; like a mantra they roll by, like a rosary, a pilgrimage, a trance. This morning their refrain contained scudding reaches over an almost black and dancing sea, and a tiny vivid rainbow repeatedly caught in spray.

5 March
Ten days out, and the plot of the collective journey is emerging (all stories need a Protagonist who has a Problem, often in the form of an Antagonist). Our Protagonist is Inga Rautenbach, head of the scientific team, who is working together with the Americans, Germans and French, to investigate the effect our southern oceans have on climate change over a ten year period. This involves deploying floats of various kinds into the sea at certain points of latitude and longitude to measure temperature, salinity and current down to levels of two thousand metres.

Our setting for the drama is the *SA Agulhas*, hired by the Germans at Antarctica to get them out before the ice gets too thick, and back to South Africa before their plane leaves on 19th March. The Germans had agreed that the *Agulhas* could be used by the scientists for research purposes on the way south as the investigation is important to the international community, and that an extra day would be granted at the Germans' expense. Now, due to bad weather, it looks as though we are to arrive at the shelf two days late, and the head of the German expedition (the Antagonist) is hopping mad, having assumed that the delay is due to the selfish arrogance of our scientists. For the past two days the air about the ship has been thick and hot with waves as emails and phone calls fly to and fro between the various parties in various continents with accusations and counter-accusations.

The Germans have insisted that any extra days be for Inga's account, so she has told the purser to put it on her bar tab (approximately R300 000). There was a suggestion that she use her married name and sunglasses when the Germans board, and that we tell them that Dr Rautenbach is no longer on the ship, that she threw herself overboard in a fit of remorse. Alternatively there is a cabin on the crew deck reserved for criminals to which she could retire. Apparently there was a murder on the maiden trip – the Bosun was stabbed to death. All the present story needs now is a love triangle and a murder to up the stakes.

Meanwhile the poor Frenchman has sunk into a huge depression. After deploying one of the expensive research floats today, he discovered he had dropped it over the only sea mount (mountain peak under the sea) we cross during the whole trip, and it therefore could not descend to the necessary depths.

We are about to cross the Antarctic Circle, whereupon it is customary for all crew and passengers who have not crossed it previously to be initiated to Neptune's mighty rule which includes, I hear, flour and eggs and very cold water as well as a slating of one's character. Having just read *Endurance* I will keep Shackleton's ordeal in mind to get me through. It all ends in a braai on deck if the weather allows.

The government pirate tells me the technical support at Antarctica must prepare a site for the off- and on-loading of supplies and people from the ship. This involves grading a ramp down through the ice shelf, which is like a cliff face, until it is low enough for the ship to dock. This is one of the most dangerous jobs in the world as the edge of the ice can give way and the grader could fall into the water. When the ship arrives, it noses into the cliff face of ice, then keeps the engines running so as to stabilise the ship while on- and off-loading using the large crane on the foredeck.

The seas are much calmer today; the night before last hardly anyone slept as the sea was so turbulent, although the purser says it can get a lot rougher. Twelve years ago a storm caused the ship to roll so much that a window on the bridge six floors up was smashed by a wave.

7 March
We are in the thick of the ice and a very surreal landscape it is, as though we have sailed somehow into a science fiction novel, with ice scraping alarmingly down the side of the ship. I have succumbed to wearing my Antarctic gear, a laborious business. I spend ages dressing and undressing. My outfit consists of thermal underwear, a layer of my own clothes, balaclava, thick woollen socks, padded and waterproofed overalls, and hooded jacket which Velcro's closed over my mouth and nose, rendering me practically blind as my glasses fog up instantly. These disabilities, together with the regulation boots, which are stiff and huge and relatively heavy, mean that I have had to learn to walk all over again, as there are many stairs (the ones outside adorned with invisible ice) that invite a fall. I discover that the first mate omitted to include gloves when I was fitted out on shore, and a young cadet, the only black person above crew level, is assigned to trawl through the stock room for an extra pair. He tells me he is from KwaZulu-Natal and rarely gets to see his family; also that he wanted to be an architect but could not afford the fees, so ended up at sea. He observes there is no ring on my finger, and admonishes me that at my age I should be married. He is further mortified to discover that the only gloves available are huge dirty leather ones, but I am immensely grateful. It is even cold indoors as the air conditioning is malfunctioning.

Last year they found a stowaway blue and shivering in a container when they were half way to Antarctica; the poor man thought he had boarded a ship headed for New York.

8 March
It was all true. We were subjected to three dunkings in a bath of water fresh from the literally icy sea, followed by an egg on the head from Neptune, then flour from Mrs Neptune who

brandished the most enormous false breasts, then a shot of antidote from the 'doctor' who dressed as though he had just emerged from a horror movie – a syringeful of Tabasco sauce.

After showering – with the water pressure hopeless thanks to all the other miscreants trying to get egg out of their hair and restore circulation to the limbs – we had a braai with the crew on the helideck; most bizarre, braaing in intermittent snow surrounded by icebergs. We made gluhwein, and I got stuck in. It was very good and warming, and I am sorry to say that I have disproved the theory that any alcohol in gluhwein boils off, and was forced to retire to my bunk.

We arrive at the ice shelf this afternoon. I'm loving this strange adventure.

9 March
Day fourteen, and we are at the shelf after crushing a path through the crust of frozen ocean, for the entire sea is encased in ice. So strange to see these thick blue/white slabs crack and shift, sliding over each other to make way for the ship, or crumbling into a trail we leave churned up behind us, a dark blue road marking this pale wilderness that soon closes over again as though we were never here. Two emperor penguins standing on the ice flapped at us as we approached, their golden heads turning this way and that to inspect the peculiarity that we are. Other penguins, their bellies streaking white beneath the freezing waters, go after fish. They hunt in packs, driving them out from under the ice into their comrades' beaks. They are living out their lives as though humans are not necessary on the planet.

The shelf is all we'll see of this strange land. The containers we must bring aboard stand around in snow like baleful cows in a British field in winter. The ship is nosed into the ice, and all crew on deck assist in loading the Germans and their cargo. We will not be allowed ashore. The Captain offers consolation: a block of Antarctic ice is stored in the freezer for me to take home on our return.

All about are icebergs run aground on the continental shelf; they hold their whiteness against the shifting colours of the sky as the sun approaches the horizon in a long gentle descent. The sunsets here last for hours, and the night is not completely dark, but bleeds a rim of red towards the south. The sky reminds us that there are colours other than the grey-scale and shades of blue in this wilderness; the algae do so too: beige or green, seen occasionally through thin plates of ice.

***

The scientists aboard and those returning from the ice have a common mission: to plot climate change historically and prospectively in order to understand better the crisis we face upon the earth. The fire of our industrial processes is accelerating the earth's tendency to change, and the polar caps are melting. Headlines received via Internet are pinned to the notice board daily; we read that in the Arctic the ice plate cracked, sending half a research base to the bottom of the sea.

***

We are fortunate in that while we have been here, watching the on- and offloading of containers and fuel, the sun has shone and the wind has been mild; nevertheless the air temperature is minus thirteen degrees. I would not last long as an Antarctic explorer; after half an hour outside in what they call the monkey house on top of the bridge, even with gloves on, my fingers are in such pain I want to shriek. Fortunately there is also a sheltered and heated lookout intended for birdwatchers, but it does very well for Inga and me as we rate the Germans working on the shore through her binoculars. She has booked one with

DAWN GARISCH

a moustache; I am forced to remind her that she's a married woman. Besides, I doubt they have forgiven her.

Last night the weatherman recorded temperatures of minus thirty-three with wind chill factored in. Even my mattress felt cold, and I wore two layers of clothing and slept under three duvets.

We leave this afternoon with conditions looking good. The sea ice does not appear too thick; with heavy snowfall in the night, the ice can rapidly thicken to over seventy centimetres and we would be in trouble. It would then require wild seas and winds to break a passage through, or a Russian icebreaker ship working nearby to get us out. The Germans have begun to board; already the atmosphere is changing, and we will have to see what this addition brings.

11 March

Day sixteen and the ship has turned back, back to the shifting sea, our mission complete, our homes once more our destination. A slash of red embedded in the ice cliff revealed itself as the thrusters pulled the bow away from the shelf. It looked like blood, like fire. The hull is repainted every year; every year it leaves this scab where the motion of the ship rubs its nose against the shelf.

In bed last night, I felt a shift that has to do with sailing to the end of the earth. It is not for nothing that we undertake these journeys. For over a hundred years humankind has sailed into these frozen lands as into a dream to find a keyhole through which we snatch a glimpse of how the gods might live; this extremity, this journey into death where life, different from the one we know, flourishes. Hardship has been integrated here until it is a substance that you walk on, as any other thing.

Throughout my life, certain writers have spoken to my core. Mindell salvaged the connection between a first dream and chronic illness; Helen Luke suggests the task of life is to discover what story you are living and to recover the images that underpin and transform that story, starting with the first remembered dream. My body dreams of inflammation, of flames that slowly smoulder patches in my vision, that crackle down my spine, inflammation raging against indifference, the icy intransigence of my body to therapies and medication. It holds fast to a course unfathomable, and I have come at last to relinquish ideas of cure, that mastiff grip on outcomes, and find myself wondering what lies beyond the blind horizon, if I allow myself to venture there, in pain and with damaged sight, accepting that I might have been looking all my life in the wrong place with inapposite tools.

Kafka said: a book must be an axe for the frozen sea within; I read this years ago with shock and recognition, for that is what they were – the books that saved my life did so by breaking me open so that mystery might enter and thereby break me open further. Not only books, but the seeds from which they spring: the words and images emerging from the salt dark, this trail of bubbles that hints of life within.

So I sit daily at my desk trying to write my way into why I am here, chipping at the keyboard until my inner ice gives way.

***

We are out of the frozen sea, barring the band of icebergs still to come, and making good time. It has been snowing, and the cadets have built a snowman on the helideck. The marine biologist and I felt it needed a response, so I earned my lunch today shovelling and moulding snow into a Godzilla, poised and about to chomp the snowman. Sadly, we couldn't find the technical support person to install flashing red eyes into the monster's head, so we made do with the red caps of cheap wine bottles salvaged from the bin.

This afternoon after my nap, I stepped out of my bunk onto a soggy carpet. Pipes are bursting throughout the ship as water frozen in them thaws. In addition, in contravention to the large notice displayed on a weather door, someone left it open and a wave washed through our level. The purser is furious, the hospital floor is under water and it is raining in the dining room. The Bosun and his right-hand man are singing as they repair the pipes. For them it is just another day at sea. I don my boots and wade into the pond sloshing around the hospital floor and help move some equipment to higher ground. The water supply is switched off for a while and some researchers resort to drinking beer. Fortunately nothing is damaged. The passages and cabin floors become adorned with towels, and after the mop up, the carpet in my cabin looks several shades cleaner.

The Germans are largely keeping to themselves. Initially we thought that they were sulking, but it transpires that most do not speak English. Inga is the only one amongst us who speaks German; she reserves this for eavesdropping to discover how much trouble she is in. Thus far the pickings are disappointing; the Germans talk to each other about technicalities, weather and movies. One young man who speaks English is eager to befriend us and sits with us at table, abandoning his compatriots altogether. He is doing his doctoral thesis on surveying the area for the new German base and reports he had a hard time both outdoors (in blizzards he had difficulty distinguishing up from down) and indoors (he did not get on with his close-range colleagues). An older man who has been to the Antarctic for five months a year for the past twenty years has been cordial; from these two we have learnt a lot:

- The present German base – one of three – is built on the ice shelf and is sinking. It is now ten metres below the surface, and moving northwards at half a metre a day, hence the need to build a new base.

- The ice cores they drill out down to two and a half kilometres deep are cut into metre lengths and transported in refrigerated containers for analysis in Germany. Once there, they are cut in half lengthwise and half are stored so that when improved methods are developed to analyse the samples, they don't have to go back and drill more out again. They have found a layer of volcanic ash of the same age spread over a quarter of Antarctica, pointing to a massive volcanic eruption some one hundred thousand years ago, probably in New Zealand.

- The interface of the ice with bedrock is at zero degrees due to the pressure of ice above and the radiant heat from earth, so the whole of the ice covering Antarctica is floating on a thin layer of water.

- Penguins contaminate the water supply as they poo everywhere, and the ice and snow must be melted and strained through expensive filters to render it fit for human consumption. The areas where the penguins are most concentrated can be seen on satellite images by the extensive hue caused by the guano.

- Build-up of static electricity due to strong winds can cause electronic equipment to fail in the bases; those bases that have sunk below the ice do not have this problem.

The German doctor is reclusive; we have only occasional sightings of her at mealtimes. For the remainder she inhabits her cabin – my abandoned, smelly one; I am convinced she is olfactorily impaired. I managed to corner her on the helideck on the first day the sun offered something more than light. The deck was suddenly full of thawing Germans, the legs of their shorts rolled up, their pale flesh inviting sunburn. She sat apart, chewing gum, focussed entirely on the heavy novel on her lap, but emerged briefly at my approach, reporting that Antarctica is a very hostile place and that humans should not go there. She believes the research interest in the continent is really to allow countries to maintain their stakes in the continent should it become feasible to mine the natural resources. She said for the first time in her life she is glad to be going back to Germany.

***

The other night I was awed by hundreds of large phosphorescent jellyfish disturbed by the wake of the ship, swirling away like underwater lights. It made me wonder about images – the signposts protruding from the expansive sea of dreams: do they persist throughout a life, constant reference points to the journey of the soul, or do they themselves transform, metamorphosing into beacons and cairns appropriate to one's developmental stage? As a child, I believed the miracle depicted in my dream that a cold wasteland would not put out my light.

I have recently emerged from fire, walking over the ice horizon of my greatest fears, the foundation of my marriage breaking up beneath me, the pain on my children's faces as I betrayed their belief that their parents would never part. I abandoned base camp which had become a pack of lies, walking on into those truths like an Antarctic blizzard tearing off my face. And still I walked, trusting that my home fire resided within me and that my sons would survive, for there must be a better way to live, a heartfelt home to return to, prodigal, having risked all to find another ending to my story.

Perhaps I have voyaged through sufficient extremity to last a while, and can enjoy the softer fruits of being human; perhaps I can trust that what has kept my light alive through frozen landscapes will not fail me now, that miracles happen every day, and that there is time for thaw, growth and greening. I look forward in this second half of life to a gently warming sun shining down on open waters, the fire of mulled wine on a cold winter's night and the soft, warm belly of my cat unfurled after sleep.

***

People are getting tired of the journey now and long for home; moods are frayed and viral illnesses abound. Shaun is irritated by Jean-Claude's table manners to the point of moving to another seat, Inga can't stand Herman's hair parting, and Herman is annoyed that Shaun has taken 'his place' at table.

The night before we dock the wine is on the house – or rather, on the ship – and I worry about the potential increase in my workload as the empty bottles line up on the table like a defeated army, and the assembled company begins to display high-risk behaviour. My concern does not last, as unbeknown to me the Frenchman keeps my one permitted glass topped up, and before long I am offering discount rates for keyhole surgery and singing experimental songs by moonlight up on the helideck.

I retain only island memories of the evening: I know the biologist cut his finger instead of his steak whereupon I talked him into receiving an anti-tetanus vaccine injection, which went quite well, considering the considerable challenge of inserting a moving object into a moving object. Inga danced with a table, which left her patched with brownish bruises.

Later an officer approached me to discuss his hernia operation and then to put to me, without my inquiry, that size doesn't matter. When he started telling me that he loved his wife, I attempted to change the subject, but he sailed on anyway, and offered me pleasure in exchange for pleasure. I wouldn't, he suggested, even have to take many clothes off.

Back in my cabin, while congratulating myself on having survived the night, I discovered Tabasco sauce on my toothbrush after inserting it into my mouth, and plastic wrap across the toilet bowl while peeing. I fell asleep wondering about men, reprisals and connections to the pleasure centre.

18 March
Day twenty-three and land is in sight, the familiar contours of home. I am struck by how these massive eruptions of earth are rooted deeply in the ocean floor, from where all life seems to

arise, and about which we know less than the surface of the moon.

Our ship at long last comes to rest, tethered like a tired horse to land, waiting to be replenished before the next voyage out. I retrieve my passport and return my Antarctic clothing. The young black cadet asks me boldly to take him to the opera next time the ship docks, as he has never been before.

My companions and I say goodbye before dispersing. The weatherman is met by his divorced wife, with whom I later hear he spent the night; an officer who has signed up for extra voyages is fetched by an unenthusiastic wife and two ambivalent daughters; a crew member whose father died while we were at sea is received by relatives in black. We are delivered back to life that has moved on, as we have.

Stepping off the gangplank to the welcome of a good friend, I find I must learn to walk again, for the earth tilts and shifts beneath my feet reminding me I am a beginner always, that what I'm used to is what I know. Tomorrow is my birthday and I want to celebrate. More than anything I want to see my sons' changed faces, to throw a party round a tub of Antarctic ice and to rest afterwards upon the dreamboat of my bed.

***

I discovered that my son had already begun to arrange a party, the first time in my adult life anyone had done this for me. The piece of Antarctica went into the freezer until the party, when few believed the ice keeping the beer cold was from the southern shelf and not from the machine at the local bottle store. When everyone had gone home and the fire round which we had sat outside had died, my son and I launched what was left of the ice into the swimming pool where it looked uncomfortable, lit by underwater lights, as though it didn't belong here.

The next morning it was gone.

***

DAWN GARISCH

PART
THREE

Tracking the Truth

15. To Trust or not to Trust

One does not discover new lands without
consenting to lose sight of the shore for a very
long time.

André Gide

We all have aspects of our lives that we would like to change.
But attempts to alter our behaviour and circumstances initially
increase anxiety; so we mostly don't unless forced to. Also, we
might not be aware of what change is possible, and what is not.

Confronting our unfounded fears might allow real concern
for ourselves, others and the earth to emerge. If we take our
courage in our hands and step out of repetitive patterns, how
do we decide on a new path? Before we examine means to
alleviate the situation, we must first dig ourselves in deeper to
investigate the full extent of the problem. We will take a closer
look at trust, and what breaks it.

A small child trusts her parents or caregivers automatically,
because she depends on them for care and sustenance for her
survival. They are her point of reference in the world, as she
knows no other, and has not yet developed the neural capacity
to question her circumstances.

A time inevitably arrives when a child experiences
betrayal by the parent. She recognises for the first time that her
parents are fallible. This constitutes a crisis, and a plunge into
fearfulness and rage. In order to overcome the betrayal, she
must relinquish the idea of perfection, and admit reality. She
has to accept that humans are fallible, and develop the ability
to discern when to trust and when not to do so. Is the parent a

'good enough' parent who is trustworthy most of the time, or is the parent mostly untrustworthy?

It is not only parents who betray our trust. At some point it occurs in any close relationship that we had hoped to depend on. Most people are trustworthy most of the time. However, we may have areas where we are predictably untrustworthy, for example people who always arrive late, or who habitually make excuses to extract themselves from arrangements, or who repeatedly pass on personal confidences.

A young male patient arrived to see me. He was shocked to discover that Dr Garisch was a woman. I assured him that all general practitioners deal with all issues, but if he was more comfortable with a male doctor, I would see whether one of my colleagues was available.

He shook his head, sat down, and plunged into a story of how, while he was away on business, he had drunk too much alcohol one night, and had sex with a woman he didn't know well. He was terrified that he had contracted a sexually transmitted disease, and that his girlfriend would find out. He had no genital or other symptoms suggestive of an STD, and the examination was normal. I counselled him and ran blood tests which were negative, and then after a few weeks I repeated the HIV test to cover the window period, which was again negative.

The man was not reassured. He returned several times during the next few months, wanting to be retested. In the interim he had developed a tight feeling in his chest and could not sleep at night. I could find no evidence of cardiac, gastrointestinal or respiratory disease. I suggested that his symptoms were of anxiety – the voice of his conscience – and reassured him that making mistakes is the most human of traits. Errors, I proposed, are in themselves not the problem, as one can make amends in most instances. The main thing is to learn from mistakes to avoid repeating them to our own detriment, and to the detriment of those we love. I suggested that he perhaps tell his girlfriend what had happened, and work it through with her. He was adamant that he could not do this because she would leave him. He declined the option of psychotherapy.

We all have an idea about who we are, but every now and then something happens that gives us a window into another aspect of our natures. This young man saw himself as faithful and reliable, and he could not forgive himself for betraying the image he had of himself. I suggested that he bring his girlfriend in if he would like me to facilitate his telling her, but he refused the offer.

I told him that any relationship will come to the point where it is tested. That is the way of life. How the two individuals involved respond to the difficulty will determine the viability or strength of the partnership longer term. I said that although it was not essential that he tell his girlfriend about this once-off betrayal, it was an opportunity to get real with each other. If not this event, then there would be others that arise in their relationship which would test it to the core.

Hillman suggests that we cannot have trust without the possibility of betrayal.[58] Whether in a love relationship, or with one's doctor, homeopath, therapist, religious leader, building contractor, divorce lawyer, dried milk producer or dentist, we might unconsciously want them to have an expertise and authority that will function like an all-powerful, consistent, infallible parent or even a god. Hillman calls this primal trust, and he likens it to the naïve, out-of-this-world trust of Adam's symbiosis with God before the Fall. We want the person we have invested with our trust to know what is best for us, look after us and always act in our best interests. When they let us down, our impulse might be towards revenge, denial of the value of the relationship, or cynicism. Or it may eventually resolve into a more conscious acceptance of an imperfect world. The relationship will never be the same after betrayal, but if worked with consciously by both parties, it can become less innocent, ignorant or self-deceptive.

Situations arise where not betraying another might mean betraying yourself. Patients who are really ill and refuse a sick note, protesting that they are needed at work, could be overriding their best interests. In a marriage, a spouse may stay in a repetitively abusive relationship because of the vow to love their partner forever.

When we are ill or injured, it can feel as though our bodies have betrayed us. We rely on our bodies to drive us around, taking them for granted until they break down at the side of the road. I have seen patients annoyed, even outraged, that they should be left in the lurch and in bed, when they have important meetings to attend.

***

In his 2005 acceptance speech[59] for the Nobel Prize for Literature, playwright Harold Pinter notes: 'There are no hard distinctions between what is real and what is unreal, nor between what is true and what is false. A thing ... can be both true and false.' His assertion applies to the exploration of reality through art. But as citizens, he argues, we must ask: What is true? What is false?

Artists, he claims, use language to probe the truth, whereas politicians 'on the evidence available to us, are interested not in truth but in power and in the maintenance of that power. To maintain that power it is essential that people ... live in ignorance of the truth, even the truth of their own lives. What surrounds us therefore is a vast tapestry of lies, upon which we feed.'

Noam Chomsky writes that the foundation of government is the control of public opinion through lies and manipulation. He points out that we recognise this strategy with ease in the most despotic and military of governments, but argues that 'it is far more important in the free societies, where obedience cannot be maintained by the lash ... The modern institutions of thought control, frankly called propaganda ... originated in the most free societies.[60]

Chomsky appeals to the public to educate itself in order to challenge the manipulations of the state to control public opinion. If we do not do this, he says, it allows for those in power to deceive, to steal from and even to destroy other countries while purporting to be advancing democracy.

***

In his Schumacher lecture entitled '... And Huge is Ugly',[61] James Hillman points to the modern trend towards enormity – from multinationals, agribusiness and supermarkets, to genocides of millions and population explosions, to mega-cities and garbage barges. He argues that burgeoning hugeness has numbed our sensitivity to beauty.

The contemporary trends in psychotherapy and the New Age movement are in danger of reducing the power of the psyche to a narcissistic obsession with the self. We persuade ourselves to trust the belief that if we turn inward, away from the mess we have created in the world, and work on ourselves to find serenity, this will contribute to improving the political and social situation in the world.

Hillman takes psychotherapists to task for turning fear, outrage, desire and shame into the neurotic individual emotions of anxiety, anger, neediness and guilt. Calling them our animal senses, he argues that they are appropriate and essential attributes for life.[62]

We need these emotions to alert ourselves to the toxic mess we are continuing to create in our own home, the world. They are guides to help us find our way. Dissociating us from these responses, and perverting them into neuroses which can then be medicated or purged, numbs us to the abuse that surrounds us and allows it to continue. We learn not to protest. Hillman states that our propensity for consumption and waste as distractions from boredom is not merely immoral and unhealthy, it is shameful.

We need to wake up to desire, not as mass-produced and mass-marketed megabuck pornography, nor as the latest 'must-haves' on the mall racks, but as the yearning for connection with the psyche, creativity, intimacy and life.

Undermining our animal instincts by calling them personal problems, we cut off an important organ of perception. This could be a major reason why we are anxious and depressed: we accept the unacceptable while knowing we are fooling ourselves. Both the world and Psyche need our outraged, ashamed, fearful and desirous engagement.

***

As adults we need to become curious about who we are and how we live. We need to question our actions and ask whether they benefit ourselves, each other and the earth, whether we have to accept and trust the way things are, and what we might do to change this. Scratching below the veneer of how we have always seen ourselves and the world can be very alarming. It can cause panic attacks and dizzy spells. We want to avoid suffering, so we are reluctant to go there.

We have constructed the rickety platform of contemporary life, and need to reconsider. The scientists and the artists have contributions to make as we stumble on, trying to find an authentic and congruent way to live.

***

16. Instruments of Truth-finding

The pursuit of truth is life-giving.

John Lukacs[63]

There is a crisis of trust in the world, with good reason. People are using the term polycrisis, as there are problems in all departments. Corruption and abuse are not the bad behaviour of a few aberrants; they are endemic all over the world, from financial scams to tax evasion to bribery of doctors to stressful working conditions to bad eating habits. We know we are being lied to about how various products will ensure the whitest teeth, popularity and relief. Our lives are littered with competing falsehoods. Our economy depends on us buying things we don't need.

It is time to examine the instruments hailed as methods to ensure that we are not being deceived. This section of the book examines whether they are dependable, or whether they have let us down.

The human brain, by its very nature, makes associations in an attempt to make sense of ourselves and the world. In other words, we are constantly, unconsciously, on the lookout for patterns. Huge areas of the brain are allocated to associative functions. Making correlations about happenings in the outside world occurs by making neural connections in the cortex. But the brain sometimes comes to false conclusions. The mind is easily tricked. Fabricated or false associations can be incorporated into the culture as general knowledge or 'common sense'; for example that butter is good for treating burns, or that the air is the only way infection is spread.

Epidemiology is a branch of science concerned with the occurrence, transmission and control of epidemic diseases. Just over two hundred years ago, Dr Alexander Gordon, an obstetrician in Aberdeen, investigated an epidemic of puerperal fever, or sepsis, in women who had recently given birth. The mortality rate of this disease is very high. At the time, people believed that the contagion was transmitted through the atmosphere. In one of the first epidemiological studies, Dr Gordon kept a diary of all women who were infected, their ages and addresses, whether they lived or died, and whether he or a midwife had assisted the delivery.

A pattern emerged, and Dr Gordon was able to conclude that the contagion was carried from one birthing room to the next on the hands and clothing of the midwives whose job it was to assist the patient and to prevent harm. The healer herself had unwittingly carried death into the heart of the home. With candour and scientific objectivity Gordon wrote in his treatise, published in 1795: 'It is a disagreeable declaration for me to mention, that I myself was the means of carrying the infection to a great number of women.'[64]

He noted: 'the observations which an extensive experience has enabled me to make will serve to illustrate ... that if practitioners had observed more and reasoned less, there would have been little dispute, either about the nature or seat of this disease.'

Observation over time is an essential aspect of the modern approach to ascertaining truth in medicine. In the next chapter we will look at the tool of scientific method more closely.

***

Marion Milner asserts that the poet – in the broad sense, including all the arts – is an essential, not a luxury.

> It was not until [man] had learnt something
> about the facts of climate and the seasons …
> that he could know how to use these to his own
> advantage and avoid being destroyed by them.
> But there were not only external facts he had
> to know. There were internal facts, facts of his
> own impulses and conflicting desires, and it was
> here that the poet was the pioneer … often, by
> not realising the nature and strength of their own
> desires, men have been wrecked by them.[65]

Art is able to illuminate internal facts of impulses and desires both in the artist and in those who experience it – readers and audiences. Powerful art pulls the bandages off our denial, and asks awkward, embarrassing, outrageous questions. It wields the cold, wet fish of reality. Or it can be the ravishing awakening to mystery and beauty, alerting us to things we take for granted every day. Art displayed in public can be a form of witnessing – of our time and its beauty, difficulties and challenges.

The courage, patience and focus of the artist can bring something of true value into being for us all to experience and recognise. The tools employed by the artist are different from those of the scientist, yet there are overlaps, as we shall see.

***

17. Tracking the Truth as a Scientist

> There are two possible outcomes: If the result confirms the hypothesis, then you've made a measurement. If the result is contrary to the hypothesis, then you've made a discovery.
>
> Enrico Fermi[66]

Last night at a dinner party, a man held forth about how ancient Arab civilization did not develop any original ideas, but stole them from the Greek and Spanish cultures that they had conquered. No matter what evidence was presented to him, he was unswayed in his belief that Arab culture is inferior.

We all have our beliefs that we have inherited or adopted that seem immune to evidence and logic. The Qur'an advises: 'You shall not accept any information, unless you verify it for yourself. I have given you the hearing, the eyesight, and the brain, and you are responsible for using them.'[67]

The first record of a person employing what we now term 'scientific method' dates back to the tenth century AD. Abū 'Alī al-Hasan ibn al-Hasan ibn al-Haytham (translated as Alhacen or Alhazen in the West), was born in Persia, now Iraq, in 965 AD. The method he proposed has come to form the backbone of contemporary culture, yet it was applied and described for the first time a mere one thousand years ago. During much of the six hundred thousand years prior to this, our species relied mainly on conjecture, association and story to explain life and the universe.

We know from oral traditions and written accounts that humans extrapolate from the evidence, often wildly. We thought that the earth was flat and stationary, the sun moved across the sky, and that illness and drought were punishments for not obeying deities, or were curses invoked by enemies. Strangers who looked, behaved or spoke differently from your tribe were denounced as either stupid and ugly, or they were elevated as the arrival of a god. War was the best method to achieve peace. Character could be determined from the shape of a person's head. Untying thongs and shoes and opening doors allowed labour to progress. The spleen was the seat of emotion. The laying on of hands cast out illness or malevolent spirits. Seizures were evidence of possession. Potions drunk at full moon could make someone fall in love with you.

Beliefs that were once common sense and common-place have frequently been overturned. Scientific method evolved as an attempt to set aside opinion, prejudice, superstition and tradition to uncover the truth. It is the process by which scientists endeavour to construct an accurate – that is, reliable, consistent and non-arbitrary – representation of the world.

However, humans have routinely applied scientific principles for centuries without knowing that that was what they were doing:

- Identifying a problem – how can I prevent this animal I have just killed from going bad before we have time to eat it?

- Testing – cut it into strips, salt it and dry it in the sun.

- Observing – the dried and salted meat does not rot.

- Repeat testing – the procedure works repeatedly.

Ibn al-Haytham formally introduced the importance of observation, testing and measurement to ascertain whether a belief was the truth. His scientific method was very similar to the modern application and consisted of the following:[68]

- Observation
- Statement of problem
- Formulation of hypothesis

- Testing of hypothesis using experimentation
- Analysis of experimental results
- Interpretation of data and formulation of conclusion
- Publication of findings

By applying these principles, he correctly refuted many long-held beliefs, for example, that the moon does not reflect sunlight like a mirror, that light is not produced by the eye but perceived by it, that the Milky Way is not part of the earth's atmosphere but is very far away, and that vision occurs in the brain, not in the eyes. He also astutely observed that people 'see' events in the world according to their experience of them, and not necessarily according to reality.

> Therefore, the seeker after the truth is not one who studies the writings of the ancients and, following his natural disposition, puts his trust in them, but rather the one who suspects his faith in them and questions what he gathers from them, the one who submits to argument and demonstration, and not to the sayings of a human being whose nature is fraught with all kinds of imperfection and deficiency. Thus the duty of the man who investigates the writings of scientists, if learning the truth is his goal, is to make himself an enemy of all that he reads, and, applying his mind to the core and margins of its content, attack it from every side. He should also suspect himself as he performs his critical examination of it, so that he may avoid falling into either prejudice or leniency.[69]

In its ideal form, science does not set out to prove a point.[3] But Ibn al-Haytham knew that science, like everything else,

---

[3] Interestingly, neither does art. 'Art' that sets out to prove a point is

including religion, is attached to people, who are attached to their psychologies.

***

Although the scientific method has been around for a thousand years, medical science has only relatively recently cottoned on. When I was trained during the years 1975 to 1981 the term 'evidence-based medicine' was not in use. We were not taught statistics, nor how to read a journal article critically. These skills are essential to try and interpret the mass of conflicting information that confronts doctors and their patients. Nowadays the medical fraternity no longer supports treatments whose merits have not been thoroughly investigated.

Twenty years before I qualified, H. K. Beecher opened a can of worms by noting in his article, 'The Powerful Placebo',[70] that a sizeable proportion of people, whom he called placebo-responders, get better when given treatments that have no physiological effects on the body. He pointed out that in order to measure the true effect of any agent, researchers had to correct for this. Beecher therefore suggested that participants be divided into two random groups, and that the treatment and placebo be packaged identically – for example in a green and white capsule. One group would get the capsule containing the substance under study, and the other would get the capsule containing the inert sugar or starch.

Two further problems arose from this recommendation. One concerned ethics: Participants in a trial need to know that this is an experiment, and that what they receive may or may not contain an active ingredient. Indeed they do – researchers explain the trial to the participants in detail before they sign informed consent. As a consequence, the efficacy of the placebo, which appears to depend on trust and faith, is diminished. If you know that the medication you are receiving might be a starch pill, it cuts across the anticipation of cure.

---

called propaganda.

The other problem, researchers noted, was that if the person administering the treatment knows whether or not it contains starch or the medication under study, subtle interactions in the consultation could cue the participant as to which substance she was ingesting. To avoid this pitfall, neither the dispenser nor the patient is allowed to know whether the capsules contain medicine or starch. This aspect of the method is termed 'double-blind'.

***

Patients often ask me whether a treatment works. A friend, they say, has recommended silver ions or kelp extract or vitamin B injections. Word of mouth, or anecdotal experience has been the basis for decisions for aeons. But impressions, subjective experience and anecdote are the very things that the scientific method aims to eliminate.

When a medical researcher wants to examine the effects of a substance, they first set an hypothesis. For example, someone might notice that when he eats nasturtium leaves, the pain of osteoarthritis in his knee goes away. To find out whether that is a coincidence, a researcher will set the hypothesis that nasturtium leaf extract will relieve the pain of osteoarthritis. She then needs to find a large number of osteoarthritic people who agree to take part in a trial. She does this by co-opting rheumatologists to help conduct the study. Once enough patients have signed up, she divides them randomly into two or three groups.

Random grouping of the participants helps to minimise any differences in the two groups. Differences in age, gender, race, health, educational level and income bracket, could affect the outcome of the test, and render the results of an expensive exercise inconclusive or even erroneous.

During the trial, the members of one group receive the extract of nasturtium leaves, and the others from the control group are given a placebo.

A third, randomly-assigned group can be given a substance proven to be effective in relieving osteoarthritic pain, for example an anti-inflammatory. The hypothesis would then state that not only is nasturtium leaf extract effective in relieving pain, but it is at least as effective as anti-inflammatories, with fewer side effects.

At set time intervals the patients involved in the trial report back to the researchers who examine and test them. If there are differences between the groups – say forty-three more people were helped by nasturtium medication than those receiving the placebo – statisticians calculate the difference to see whether it might reflect a natural variation, or whether we can confidently say that nasturtium leaves are in fact medicinal.

Researchers will also look at unwanted effects, for example, whether there is an increase in the incidence of heart attacks in people taking nasturtium leaf extract for arthritis.

The findings, both positive and negative, need to be written up in a standard way, where the hypothesis, method, findings and conclusions are spelt out. The article is submitted to a peer-review journal, where it is published if it is sound. The researchers must store the data generated by the study in such a way that other researchers can access them so that they can repeat the experiment to check the results. Fraudulent studies have been uncovered in this way, as well as studies that have had built-in errors which yielded incorrect conclusions.

This systematic and rigorous approach to uncovering the truth as to whether a substance will heal or harm or do nothing at all is a huge advance over an unscrupulous salesman arriving at your door and convincing you that a bottle of his proverbial snake oil can cure everything from corns to asthma. Yet many people use treatments that have not been verified by scientific method, and claim that they work.

***

DAWN GARISCH

The jury is still out as to what the placebo effect actually is, and even whether it exists. Some researchers say that measurable improvement while on a placebo could represent the natural course of the illness, where the body tends to get better anyway. Others claim that the effects are so powerful that we should be investigating the placebo rather than drugs. Newman[71] has coined the phrase 'placebo paradox', in which he points out that it is unethical to use a treatment that has no known effects in the body, but it is also unethical not to use something that heals.

The debate that rages around the placebo effect illustrates an important point. Sometimes our methods of measurement reveal something we can rely on, and sometimes they don't. The world, it seems, does not always obey the tenets of a tape measure.

***

18. Buying Health, Trading in Illness

To say that a man is made up of certain chemical elements is a satisfactory description only for those who intend to use him as a fertilizer.

Hermann Joseph Muller[72]

Health care has become big business, where many interested parties make enormous profits. Most people get sick or injured many times in their lives, or else have chronic complaints that can be alleviated by medication. In the article 'Drug Companies & Doctors: A Story of Corruption', Dr Marcia Angell, who for two decades was an editor of the *New England Journal of Medicine*, points out that: 'Even when changes of lifestyle would be more effective, doctors and their patients often believe that for every ailment and discontent there is a drug.' She continues: 'Physicians learn to practice a very drug-intensive style of medicine.'[73]

Drug companies that finance research into new medications and drug trials need to make returns on their investments. Angell shows how easy it is for researchers to manipulate data in order to demonstrate that the medicine being tested is superior to the placebo or another medicine used in the same disease.

Angell adds: 'Physicians are also led to believe that the newest, most expensive brand-name drugs are superior to older drugs or generics, even though there is seldom any evidence to that effect because sponsors do not usually compare their drugs with older drugs at equivalent doses.'[74]

Recently, there has been an explosion of new drugs on the market, many of them presenting no major advance on the old tried and trusted medicines. Pharmaceutical companies compete against each other for the position of 'market leader'. Sometimes drug reps are even made to compete within the same company, marketing the identical product under a different name and in different packaging, all in an effort to claim a bigger slice of the pie.

Doctors are approached daily by drug representatives who arrive in expensive cars bearing 'gifts' and food as an incentive for the busy general practitioner to take time out to listen to the sales pitch. These can be as embarrassing as the 'gift' of a shampoo and conditioner to illustrate the synergistic action of combination therapy, firelighters to remind the GP about treatment for erectile dysfunction, or a mug with a picture of a caveman dragging a cavewoman along by her hair, illustrating a use for an anti-inflammatory. The drug rep may literally plead with the doctor to support her by prescribing the product she is promoting. Her income depends on it. The ill patient disappears into a theoretical point on a graph where the points plotted may or may not have been manipulated into position.

South African medical practitioners are obliged by law to obtain thirty continuing medical education (CME) points each year to ensure that they stay up to date with developments in the medical field. Drug companies use this as a way to promote their products. They entice doctors, who are tired at the end of a busy day, to attend CME lectures by including meals at expensive restaurants, or even flying doctors to a hotel where they will put them up and fête them for a weekend. The doctor obtains the necessary points, sometimes learns important information, and gets to feel special and cared for. In return for hosting and toasting doctors, the drug company hopes to change their prescribing habits.

Some doctors feel that this wining and dining is a justified perk. A doctor's income, unlike that of a successful businessman, is linked to time on the job. Very few doctors refuse these bribes. I tread a wary compromise, trying not to be influenced by any consideration other than what is best for my patients. I attend the lectures and eat the food, but I pass the 'gifts' on to my domestic worker for redistribution. It amuses me to think of designer water bottles, Weber braais, wall clocks, beach towels, blankets, Leatherman tool sets, deck chairs and umbrellas, all sporting the names of pharmaceutical products, finding homes in the townships.

Speakers at CME talks receive huge financial rewards for lecturing, usually on subjects allied to products. Dr Angell points out: 'After much unfavourable publicity, medical schools and professional organizations are beginning to talk about controlling conflicts of interest, but so far the response has been tepid. They consistently refer to "potential" conflicts of interest as though that were different from the real thing, and about disclosing and "managing" them, not about prohibiting them. In short, there seems to be a desire to eliminate the smell of corruption, while keeping the money.'[75]

These practices have fostered distrust of both science and the medical establishment.

Dr Angell, referring to the book *On The Take: How Medicine's Complicity With Big Business Can Endanger Your Health*, argues that although the drug companies go to perverse excesses to promote their product, they are mostly within their mandate in the capitalist system. They are required to make as much profit as they can by whatever legal means are at their disposal on behalf of their shareholders. She does, however, cite several cases where drug companies were made to pay huge fines running to millions and even billions of dollars for fraudulent claims. Yet this was an insignificant amount compared with the enormous profits generated by false advertising and the resultant ongoing misperception of the public and doctors.

However, she argues, the medical profession does not have the excuses of business in that we are not answerable to shareholders. A physician's responsibility is to put a patient's wellbeing first. Where this duty has been tainted or subverted by pecuniary considerations, she says, the doctors should be held more accountable for their behaviour than the pharmaceutical companies.

I recently went on one of these extravaganzas in Johannesburg. At least six hundred doctors from all over South Africa attended. I learnt a lot from the lectures, which will benefit my patients, but I was acutely aware that everything, from the plane ticket to the hotel room and banquet with cabaret, comedian and musicians, was paid for by the profits made by selling medication to the sick or to those wanting to ward off illness and disability. On one hand I am grateful to the drug company that hosted an event where in one weekend I earned half a year's worth of CME points, but I felt very queasy. I, too, am culpable.

What interests me is that some doctors with whom I broached the subject of bribery and corruption looked puzzled. They looked at me as though I were a bit weird in the head. They promptly changed the subject.

Back home, I discussed the matter with a colleague who I know is critical of the pharmaceutical industry's ploys. He pointed out that it used to be much worse, before the government passed legislation limiting the excesses. Back in the 'good old days', drug reps flew doctors and their spouses to game reserves in private jets, and bought new tyres for doctors' cars. As a drug rep told me, back in those days they would do almost anything to persuade a doctor to prescribe their product preferentially.

This is how crazy it gets: a company that manufactures medication for indigestion offered surgeons and their partners a trip down the Orange River, while a rival company offered surgical couples a weekend flight to Johannesburg to see a rugby final. After these outrageous bribes, which product would they prescribe one wonders? The competing products are essentially the same.

This is one of the reasons why health insurance is so expensive. The medical aids must know that this is happening, yet they don't protest. Deceit and deficiencies are embedded in the matrix of our society. It is so pervasive, it is passed off as normal.

19. Seeing and Believing

… humanity / in gloves / and chains.

Mxolisi Nyezwa[76]

Scientific method has led to evidence-based medicine (EBM). EBM is the practice of medicine using only those investigations and treatments that researchers have proved are valid. The intention is to provide reliable information from which clinicians and patients can decide on the best solutions for health problems. This is an excellent goal. No-one would want an out-dated treatment if there is a better option available.

EBM straddles several crucial questions:

- Does the treatment do any good?
- Does it do harm?
- Does it do significant good, and is the harm minor?
- Is it an advance over what is already available?

At first glance, this might appear a simple matter, but it is not. There is an art in research to answering these questions truthfully. There are many ways a study can founder. If it does, all the time, effort and money spent can come to nothing. Even worse, if no-one picks up the error, false results might be incorporated into policy or guidelines, which can affect the health and general welfare of millions of people. The responsibility to yield accurate findings is enormous.

In 1993, specialist groups convened to draw up guidelines to eliminate errors in drug trials. The Consolidated Standards of Reporting Trials (CONSORT) has a checklist of twenty-two items to assess the quality of randomised controlled trials, or RCT.

Bausell[77] offers some simpler criteria that rule out the worst offenders:

- Subjects must be randomly assigned
- At least fifty subjects per group
- Less than twenty-five per cent dropout rate
- Publication in a high-quality, prestigious, peer-reviewed journal

Ideally, those who engage in research do it because they are curious about how and whether something works and because they care about the betterment of humankind. But the temptation to fiddle results or 'massage' the data not only stems from those who stand to gain financially from a positive result. Researchers are under enormous pressure to publish. At stake are their chances for securing promotion as well as funds for future research. Some need to please their bosses, or to finish their degrees, or add a line to their CVs so as to market themselves.

For a doctor to keep up with the latest findings, and to sort out which are relevant and reliable, is a nightmare. Over two million articles relevant to medical practice are published every year. To keep abreast of discoveries in their field alone, doctors would have to read nineteen articles a day. This is impossible; instead, they read meta-analyses – overviews of all the recent studies looking at, for example, the treatment of osteoporosis.

The authors conducting the meta-analysis search for all articles on the subject published within a certain time frame. Editors are supposed to scrutinise articles before they publish to check whether the researchers used sound methods. Yet meta-analyses regularly report that they had to exclude studies with faulty design. When one considers the time, effort and expense involved in conducting studies, and how many are shown to be invalid, it is a shocking waste.

Even when studies are sound, this does not guarantee publication. The meta-analysis of trials looking at twelve antidepressants found that antidepressants were more effective than a placebo. On closer scrutiny, many studies showing that antidepressants had no advantage over a placebo had not been published, thus skewing the perception of doctors and the public.

The authors of this meta-analysis concluded: 'We cannot determine whether the bias observed resulted from a failure to submit manuscripts on the part of authors and sponsors, from decisions by journal editors and reviewers not to publish, or both. Selective reporting of clinical trial results may have adverse consequences for researchers, study participants, health care professionals, and patients.'[78]

***

In a recent and damning case, a new non-steroidal anti-inflammatory drug (NSAID), rofecoxib, was marketed as a major advance over the older NSAIDs. The manufacturers claimed that the new medication was not only more effective, but that it caused fewer side effects. Encouraged by the hype, and anxious to avoid the side effects of gastro-intestinal haemorrhage in their patients, doctors prescribed the wonder drug in truck loads.

My colleagues and I were shocked when rofecoxib was withdrawn from the market due to convincing evidence that its use had caused cardiovascular disability and death in users at a significantly higher rate than that of the general population. Even more reprehensible is that the authors of the original study failed to represent accurately the adverse effects on the heart that had emerged during the trial.[79]

Evidence can be problematic for reasons other than corruption. An example: there is clear evidence to treat a patient who has a stroke caused by a clot to the brain. If he receives intravenous medication to dissolve the clot and restore blood circulation, he has a much greater chance of complete recovery than if he does not receive it. But we also know that he has a small but significantly increased chance of dying of a bleed into the brain caused by that same medication. Science cannot tell you on which side of the line you will fall.

Another reason why a well-conducted trial might not yield trustworthy recommendations is that there are strict rules about excluding participants. Researchers set up trials to investigate whether one specific treatment will yield one measurable result. They frequently exclude children, the elderly, and anyone who has any disease other than the one under study.

In the real world we need answers that apply to everyone. Real people can have more than one condition, and this might impact on the drug's efficacy or toxicity. An oral vaccine like polio drops might be poorly absorbed by a child with a gastrointestinal disease. Or someone on treatment for heart failure might respond differently to someone who is not, when exposed to a new drug. Research settings do not mirror the real world.

In the UK, the National Institute for Health and Clinical Excellence (NICE) helps medical practitioners through this minefield. The chairperson, Professor Rawlins, is of the opinion that: 'Randomised controlled trials (RCTs), long regarded as the "gold standard" of evidence, have been put on an undeserved pedestal.' He says that their appearance at the top of 'hierarchies' of evidence is inappropriate; and 'hierarchies, themselves, are illusory tools for assessing evidence [and] should be replaced by a diversity of approaches that involve analysing the totality of the evidence-base.'[80]

Jeffrey Bland, medical doctor and faculty member of the Institute of Functional Medicine, suggests a different model for evaluating a therapy's safety and effectiveness, derived from systems biology. Rather than attempting to control for all differences between two populations being studied, so as to assess the role of one intervention, this model allows for study participants to engage in real world activities of daily living.

Through the computing power of the twenty-first century, the captured complex data sets can be assessed using pattern recognition and cluster analysis.[81]

In brief, he is describing a dynamic way where the idiosyncrasies of an individual on any treatment can be evaluated as to whether he is benefiting. In the future the cumbersome, expensive, drawn-out and restrictive approach of traditional EBM must give way to another more inclusive and useful method of finding out whether care is effective or not.

Bland recommends that doctors listen to the patient's story in order to develop a response to it: 'The approach to complex systems might be much more profound than just trying to pound a round peg into a square hole and get a singular diagnosis.'

***

Scientists change their recommendations as new evidence comes to light. For years we told patients that egg yolks contain too much cholesterol, and that it was unhealthy to eat more than an egg or two a week, particularly if you have a disorder of fat metabolism. We have since discovered that the cholesterol in egg is a kind that is not well absorbed by the human intestine. We are back to eating eggs every day if we want to, and the scientists have egg on their faces.

When scientists 'change their minds', it is easy for people reading the newspaper to discount medical advice as arbitrary. The problem with these criticisms, essential as they are, is that they lead some people to an undifferentiated distrust of things scientific. The baby is out, along with the bathwater.

***

20. Sickness and Health

If this desire to sacrifice my own wants was
so strong, I was faced with the paradox that
perhaps what I wanted most to do was not to do
what I most wanted to do. I knew many people
of whom this seemed true, as soon as they had
a moment to themselves free from obligations,
they would rush off to find another obligation,
someone else or something else to sacrifice their
lives to … I noticed that these same people very
often had periods of recurrent illness when they
were forced to attend to themselves.

Marion Milner[82]

Penicillin, the first manufactured antibiotic, was formally discovered a mere seventy years ago by Alexander Fleming. Antibiotics are substances that kill or inhibit the growth of bacteria. This discovery was a major advance, in that people who developed severe infections such as pneumonia, septicaemia, mastoiditis, pyelonephritis, diverticulitis, peritonitis, cellulitis, meningitis, and sexually transmitted diseases, which in many cases would result in death or severe disability, could now be helped to recover fully.

Even in those days Fleming recognised that antibiotic resistance was a potential problem, and he cautioned against indiscriminate use. Despite this, both doctors and patients have come to regard antibiotics as a quick fix, even using them when it is obvious that an infection is viral (I know it is going to go to my chest, doctor; it always does if I don't get an antibiotic).

At a recent conference, a chest physician lectured us on the increasing problem of antibiotic resistance. This will present a serious challenge in the time of our children and grandchildren. One of his recommendations is that doctors should only script antibiotics after ten days of symptoms in sinusitis, throat and ear infections, unless the patient is deteriorating.

What this physician is prescribing is the age-old remedy called the tincture of time. He is reminding us that not all bacterial infections require antibiotics. He is suggesting that the GP dispense reassurance. But many patients come to their doctor expecting to receive something more tangible than that. The doctor is the keeper of the goodies, and they want some.

Many of my patients lose patience after only two or three days of illness. Ten days away from work, sport and the busy routine of life feels too out of control. They tell me they 'can't afford' to be off work. There is nobody to take their place when they are off sick, so the work-load just mounts up, and is still there on their return. They are at breaking point, which is a major reason why they are ill in the first place, yet they see illness as further complicating their busy schedule.

***

Both the health industry and the New Age movement recommend that we strive for health, wholeness, wellness, centredness and living a well-balanced life. This book too might stop at that. It may seem like a good idea, but on closer examination, this approach excludes suffering and death. Having wellness as a focus can feed our denial. We forget that one day our flesh will decay back into the earth. We forget that our bodies are groaning under the strain of the contemporary mode of living.

If we are interested in the truth about life, we need to question whether it is symptom-free. I am grateful that we have remedies to help people who carry more physical and mental anguish than they should have to bear, yet I question the modern idea that life should flow smoothly, that problems should be vanquished as soon as possible, and that everything can be fixed with a pill. Slowing down, going to bed, withdrawing a while from the bustle of society, paying attention to the inner rather than the outer – these could have benefits not immediately apparent.

Illness and disability, like most other crises, stop us in our tracks. They force us to pay attention to our bodies and our inner reality. In bed, or hobbling round, we are taken out of the collective and forced into the margins of life. We are no longer productive or useful, and so we become failures in our own or in society's eyes. We are left with a cup of tea while others rush back to their obligations. We are left alone.

Artists, other than those in theatre or dance, have to be alone. There are artists whose aloneness has been accentuated by chronic illness, and who have harnessed their suffering in service to their art. Frida Kahlo, for example, had polio at six and later a tram accident left her leg and spine injured, resulting in thirty operations. Her self-portraits gave her a means to express these experiences, and to develop the images of her wounded and courageous life.

Jung suggests that being alone is the primary doorway into one's own being. 'I know from experience that all coercion – be it suggestion, insinuation, or any other method of persuasion – ultimately proves to be nothing but an obstacle to the highest and most decisive experience of all, which is to be alone … The patient must be alone if he is to find out what it is that supports him when he can no longer support himself. Only this experience can give him an indestructible foundation.'[83]

***

If finding out who you are and what it is you need to do while on this earth is a worthy quest, it is one that is very likely to lead you astray from the norm. As children, we take so many things for granted. Our brains and outlook are shaped largely by the beliefs, attitudes and environment we were brought up in. If the human spirit were simple, we would all fall into line and live happily ever after. But, even within a relatively homogenous group that has the same outlook and goals, there always emerges some impetus to tip the status quo. It seems that humans are inherently curious and challenging beings. Whether it is stamped into our genetic code or propelled by spirit, we look for information outside the known. Often that brings us into conflict with the established ways of doing things.

Programmes and interventions based on achieving peace have never worked for long. Peace is a temporary state which might be achieved briefly when a conflict is resolved, before the next challenge arises. For peace to be a steady state, it implies that those who disagree with the dominant ideology or situation must find a way to be compliant and not rock the boat, which will at the very least set up conflict within themselves.

People are interested in conflict. We know this because the basis for a good story is: 'there is a person who has a problem'.

Joseph Campbell's book, *The Hero With a Thousand Faces*[84] looks at myths and stories across time and culture, and identifies common aspects of the journey that the central character, or hero, takes to reach his or her goal. Heroes sometimes do not reach their goals, or reach a different goal than the one they set out towards. Heroes can unwittingly set out on a course of action, or have a crisis thrust upon them. Often the protagonist first has to overcome something in herself before she is able to overcome the external difficulty.

Stories are the earliest way that humans tried to make sense of the world, who we are, why we are here, and what we are supposed to do about it. Handed down the generations, stories impart information about life and how to live it. We read because we want to find out how other people have messed up their lives, and what happened next. Any story that does not deal with human imperfection will not have a large print run, if it gets printed at all.

Illness and accident are disruptions of peace or the norm. They are motive forces, even as they confine you to bed. They are part of what inspires the hero's journey.

***

We might declare that we want to 'be normal'. But 'normality' is merely one of many ways of being and behaving; it means middle of the road, average, or median.

There is a place and a time for choosing normality, but if you are to fulfil your unique potential, you are going to follow some private impulse and end up out on a limb, out on your very own branch, far from centre and the collective, and overhanging the terrifying abyss.

Mindell claims that chronic illness is one of the means through which the motif of your life is revealed.[85] Illness, by interrupting your own or your culture's preconceived ideas about which direction to pursue, can lead you away from what's 'normal', and into your own version of a life well lived.

The psychoanalyst Lyn Cowan[86] suggests that striving for wholeness (implying health and harmony) and balance is a kind of madness. She says the idea that it is possible for humans to attain a state as symmetrical as a mandala is a self-deception. She points out that unique expression is eccentric – it is not an idealised sphere. It is a wholeness that is asymmetrical. 'He is a real character', we say of someone who sticks out in the crowd – not because of fame or status or riches, but merely because he is not afraid to be entirely himself. So it should be. We should all be real characters in the stories of our lives.

Wholeness as a mass-marketed idea increases the pressure on us to reach an unattainable perfection. It provides a lever for businesses to get us to hand over money to acquire the latest machine, tonic or pill in the uncritical quest for health. Alternatively, we might live a wholeness that implies integrity, encompassing all that it is to be human, including the mess and discomfort of death and illness.

What a dilemma. Here I am, a medical doctor, recommending illness and death as indispensable. I have a strong urge to look over my shoulder. Could such a blasphemy get me struck off the roll?

***

Buddhists encourage cognizance of our mortality, with the saying: Death sits on your shoulder. A surprising number of people consider that talking or thinking about death is a morbid preoccupation. Being aware that we will die might well fuel anxiety, or else it can alert us that our time here is precious.

If we were able to banish death and its servants, disease and accident, what would the world look like? Without death, there would be no disintegration towards compost, and the cycle of life would shut down. We would wander the earth like Midas, our clever fingers turning everything into beautiful, durable, indigestible gold.

If we were able to control what happens, the unforeseeable would disappear. We would live within the constraints of our limited view of how things should be. We would never be able to surprise ourselves, or be surprised by information we need in order to review our lives. In doing away with the unpredictability of pain and suffering, we would also destroy what Hyde calls the happiness of happenstance.[87]

A patient who worked long hours and flew regularly around the world in an important academic job, was diagnosed recently with cancer. After surgery she went for a session of Reiki. The practitioner asked her, 'Now your body has arrested you, how do you see your new self?'

She got it. Her body had sent out a distress signal, and she took it seriously. She decided to take the rest of the year off and get more exercise, eat better and spend time doing more relaxing things. She now restricts her work to being the person who develops ideas in her field, and delegates the actual work, meetings and teaching commitments to others.

Her life has improved and her body feels better than it has for a long time.

Grateful. Serene.

A patient, who had a mastectomy for breast cancer, told me that contracting this intimate, life-threatening illness has had unexpected consequences. She has discovered strengths in herself that she has never acknowledged. It has also given the suffering she has experienced her whole life due to family circumstances a concrete and validating form. For the first time she feels that her suffering is visible to others, and has come to realise that people care about her and are there for her. Her illness has helped her allow herself to be vulnerable and to accept support and love from friends and colleagues.

As a consequence, she has become more visible. She no longer unconsciously chooses a background and peripheral position in gatherings, but has the confidence to participate more.

It could have gone the other way. Such a misfortune might have caused her to collapse in on herself and to become unhappier and more reclusive. It appears that we cannot predict how things are going to turn out, nor affix a single meaning or outcome to a single event.

During my midlife crisis, I was so out of my mind with stress that my eyesight began deteriorating. I knew that for over two years I had tried everything in my ability to solve my marital problems. It came to me, coldly and clearly, that I had reached the point where I had to choose between my eyesight and my marriage. My illness helped me take one of the hardest steps in my life. My eyes cleared, and they have not troubled me again since.

***

21. Truth and the Artist

The prayer of five stones –
Kabul, Gaza, New York City, Somalia, Jerusalem.
There is a prayer that changes the world.
I can't remember it.
The sound of water is what I think.

Christina M. Coates[88]

We feel recognition, animation and new alignment when we stand in front of a painting or sculpture that moves us, read a poem or hear music that resonates, or watch an extraordinary dance or theatre performance. What aspects of the truth do artists capture and distil and how do they do this?

Art operates through presenting a juxtaposition of ideas, words or images in a way that stimulates and affects our emotion and intellect. It has the potential to convey a complex of truths in layered ways. When performance artist Marina Abramović stood passively in a gallery as a work of art entitled *Rhythm 0*, 1974, she was testing and subverting the relationship between performer and audience. On a table nearby were 72 objects that the audience were informed they could use in any way that they chose. Some objects could give pleasure, while others could inflict pain, or even harm. Among them were a rose, a feather, honey, a whip, scissors, a scalpel, a gun and a single bullet. Initially people reacted with caution and consideration, but as time passed people began to be more aggressive, taking off her clothes and even cutting her lightly and pressing the gun against her head.

In this piece, Abramović evoked disquieting and contradictory responses: vulnerability, abuse of women, women as victims, shame, violence, provocation, guilt, protection, fear, shock and fury. She held a mirror up to our denial, co-dependency and sado-masochism.

Through its use of image, art can also connect us to the symbolic layer of life. It returns us to our poetic base – to the roots of existence when humans had not yet become alienated from the rest of life on earth. Art can thereby heal the splits between mind and body, ego and psyche, subject and object, humans and nature, sacred and profane. It can restore mystery and awe.

Or not. Art may function by stressing us through widening the fissures and forcing our gaze into the void.

Either way, we are affected, woken up, realigned. We come away changed, with a new appreciation of something that can only be translated into words with difficulty.

***

Lyn Cowan[89] argues that the relationship between the ego and the unconscious is akin to Alice encountering Wonderland. In Wonderland, or in the unconscious, the rules of analytical, deductive and empirical logic do not apply, yet Wonderland is coherent if accepted on its own terms. When the White Queen announces 'The rule is, jam tomorrow and jam yesterday – but never jam today', the logician in us objects, but the inner poet understands implicitly.

When an artist embarks on a project, it can feel something like Alice entering Wonderland. A disturbance arrives in my body pressurising me to put pen to paper in an attempt to translate the feeling into words. The discomfort is not altogether unpleasant, but it is a heightened state, or agitation. It contains the element of conflict and conflict is unsettling. By its nature conflict either goes round in circles, or it spirals in towards some kind of resolution.

This tension is usually accompanied by an image. When I start tracking this image, I don't know where the project is going, other than that it probably relates to certain universal concerns that have distilled themselves into my life and into my writing. I suspect that most artists are busy gnawing away at the same bone most of their lives from different perspectives, getting closer and closer to the marrow. Solving the problem of the novel makes me examine closely what is true in myself and, by extrapolation, in humanity.

At the very least a creative act can be a helpful container. It can give form and shape to a vague sense of distress. A difficult emotion can be transferred from the creator to the artwork. Anthony Storr, psychoanalyst and writer, proposes that anything which lessens distress in the midst of chaos, or which increases our sense of control and mastery, gives pleasure.[90]

The artwork revealing itself through your body is a result of an exquisitely terrifying subliminal conversation between the known and the unknown. Aaron Copland, musician and composer, says that he creates in order to know himself, and as each new work is only a part-answer to the question 'Who am I?', it stimulates him to pursue other and different part-answers.[91]

I have boxes of scraps and journals, and computer files full of all kinds of writing. Looking back on what I was thinking and feeling ten or twenty years ago is a gift to myself. It allows for a more nuanced reflection, and perhaps a more compassionate understanding of who I am, what I have been through and where I am up to. Writing has set me on a journey towards, instead of away from, myself.

The making of art can act as witness. One of the most valuable aspects of a long-term relationship, like a marriage or a best friendship, is that another person bears witness to your life, as you do to theirs. The most important long-term relationship we have is with ourselves, and art is a way of bearing witness to the truth of our own lives – documenting the complexity and patterns of this undertaking to live well.

Making art for oneself is one thing; publishing, exhibiting, and producing your work for the public is another. Even showing a friend or posting something on the Internet is a kind of publishing. Art displayed in public can also be a form of witnessing – of our time and its beauty, difficulties and challenges.

***

Children are born curious, and begin their lives exploring, pulling things apart and trying to put them together again. They draw, act, dance and sing. They try things out, for that is how they learn how things work and what they can rely on. They begin life without the fear of making mistakes. We think to ourselves: how cute, and laugh at the errors of children, for most of us have long since lost that unselfconscious capacity.

Art reconnects us with this spirit of curiosity and discovery, and at the same time it forges new connections in the brain. It assists us in overcoming fear of our potential and fear of error when we discover that our 'mistakes' sometimes allow our best work in.

Losing our curiosity and creativity early on in life disables us. It is like losing a sensory organ. We stumble around, half-blind, partially deaf. When we reclaim that which was meant to be ours, we can live more expansively, and be more fully and truly who we are.

***

The muse is an old religious idea: that the goddess of creativity has come to inhabit and assist you. It contains the notion that human beings and the gods need each other. A person needs inspiration from the gods, and the gods need a human being to execute the task and commit the project to paper, instrument, canvas or the dance floor.

It is possible that our brains trick us by constructing the sensation of the muse. Yet this possibility does not adequately explain some of the things that have happened to me that are tantamount to guidance.

When I started writing *Trespass*, I knew it had to be situated post-World War II for reasons of the plot, so I randomly decided that the events of the novel would take place from early 1955 to late 1956.

Twenty pages into the book, I checked what was going on in South Africa at that time so as to better situate the novel. I discovered that the only two all-women's political movements in the history of South Africa arose during the time span of the novel. The Black Sash started their campaign in 1955. Their initial cause was to protest against the Nationalist government's strategy to load the senate and thereby push through a law to take the vote away from coloured men. The following year, the African National Congress Women's League marched on the Union Buildings, protesting the new pass laws for black women. Both these extraordinary events epitomised how oppressed women might stand against abuse – feeding directly into the concerns of the novel.

A scientist might argue that I had once known and then forgotten these dates, and that, at the beginning of the project, I had chosen them unconsciously. It is possible, but I did not take history at high school, and my recall of dates is appalling.

If the muse exists, then I believe it is essential to be available to her spirit and intention. In author Barbara Kingsolver's words we need to be ready to catch the apple when it falls.[92] Without our conscious assistance, to continue her metaphor, the muse's gifts just roll away unnoticed to rot.

***

There are stories in any family or culture that are true, but that may not be told. Despite this, there are those who are prepared to tell them. Leslie Marmon Silko, in her novel *Ceremony*, and Maxine Hong Kingston in *The Woman Warrior*, broke family and cultural secrets by putting them into print. They were lauded by some and criticised by others for doing so. Thando Mgqolozana's novel *A Man Who Is Not A Man* breaks with Xhosa tradition which stipulates that those who have been initiated into manhood may not speak to women nor to those who have not been initiated about what they have been through. Lewis Hyde, in *Trickster Makes This World*, comments that social anthropologists who studied cultures from a distance often misinterpreted what they saw, as many cultures guarded themselves around strangers, not allowing them into their story.

Which stories cannot be told? Who owns a story anyway; who is its guardian? Is breaking with tradition or breaking taboos good and helpful? When is it not?

The writers who have spoken to my core are those who have revealed something about life or themselves which concerns the truth of imagination or experience, however beautiful or difficult. Many of these writers have addressed topics that have crossed private or cultural boundaries, and provided glimpses into intimate lives. These shared experiences have encouraged me, and shown me a way through in my life and in my writing. But I understand the concern about the danger of exposing what is private or sacred. Revelation carries the risk of misinterpretation, loss of identity, betrayal and shame.

A poet, preparing to interview me about the novel *Trespass*, emailed me the following: 'Reading Phyllis's thoughts is cathartic and frightening at the same time, because, although she blurs the line between madness and reality, she also speaks the truth. And thinks out loud what many of us dare not say. Is truth-telling important to you as a writer?'

My response: 'Well, there are things one can only admit to oneself, then there are things one is prepared to write down in a journal, knowing that there is a possibility it might fall into someone else's hands, and there are things one can say out loud to others. These are all different selves, with censors posted in the gateways. And of course there are the aspects of self that everyone but you can see. I am interested in working with all these truths, how they can even contradict each other.'

There are those truths that I could write, but decide not to. Not now. The ego can encourage one to make decisions that could have unfortunate consequences.

***

There is a paradox in claiming that a novel or art work can reveal the truth. After all, these are fictions. A story is fabricated, although it might be based on a true event, or cobbled together out of real incidents and actual characters. Artists borrow endlessly from life.

A work of fiction is true if it is well told, delves unflinchingly into the heart of the human condition, and then comes up with a resolution that does not cheat life, nor the reader, but wakes us up to ourselves. It is true as in 'it rings true' as is said of bells that have been cast without flaw, and sound with great beauty. It is a lovely paradox that through the manipulation of a text and thereby the reader, a truth can be revealed.

***

22. Truth-finding Tools of the Artist

If you are too sentimental or conventional for your crystals
ever to be knocked out of place
the poems you prefer will be sentimental and conventional
probably in tight little rooms
(room = stanza, in Italian, no doubt someone will explain)
with a witty bit left hanging which could be anyone's
do not disturb sign
(you never know what's going on in there)

Joan Metelerkamp[93]

In a collection of her published interviews,[94] Doris Lessing said that a novel is a problem to be solved. Something must be worked out, or worked through. This puzzle starts at the writer's desk, and if the issues in the book are resolved satisfactorily for the author, even if there are no happy endings, the reader will usually feel satisfied as well.

The difficulty for the author does not only lie in the narrative, or storyline. It is embedded in all the layers of creating the piece. There are the questions of voice, language and style, of form and content. Problems of character and dialogue, of pacing and the shape of scenes, of beginnings and middles and endings. Tensions between the personal and the political, background and foreground, tragedy and comedy.

At the heart of a novel will be a concern that is not random. The writer is embroiled in the subject matter precisely because it originally resides in her own heart. The novel is a vehicle for the author to probe and explore this terrain, not as propaganda, but as an open-ended question. In writing that ventures below the surface, as in living deeply, there are no easy answers. Engaging with the unresolved questions posed by the novel requires the novelist to engage with undecided or disturbed parts of herself. E.L. Doctorow claimed that writers hazard themselves, as every time they compose a book the composition of themselves is at stake.[95]

Working on a story inevitably brings me face to face with problems to do with the process of writing in addition to the content – my impatience and my 'drivenness', my self-doubt and my over-confidence, my fear of exposing myself and the imperative to push boundaries. How will I know whether I am stumbling down a dead-end in the story, or whether my mounting anxiety is instead about entering a dark alley to find the elusive ingredient necessary to help resolution?

My script editor for the edutainment series *Soul City* taught me that when you write a script, the first two minutes of screen time must contain a 'hook' – some moment that grabs a viewer's attention. Movies are either made for TV, or they end up there, where viewers can switch channels if they are not rapidly engaged.

The device of the hook presents a tension in the story and thereby in the reader. It entices us by making us want to know what is going to happen next. We want to see how things will turn out. We are asking ourselves: What would I do in that situation?

Stories that work do so because they speak to who we are, what we desire and what we wish to avoid. Life provides many dilemmas. So we are interested in how other people, fictional or real, track the truth or, at least, how human beings manage the complexities of life.

When I start reading a good book, I look forward to the delight of immersion in well-crafted language, characters and scenarios. I also anticipate the pleasure of having my disquietude relieved when the difficulty presented in the opening chapters of the novel is resolved by the end.

Or not. A book might end with the main character, or protagonist, unable to develop what is needed to meet a challenge. The anti-hero might circle round and round within the prison of what is familiar, repeating mistakes and digging himself in deeper. We all know people like that. We all know that feeling ourselves. The value of a stuck character is that she can stimulate our own desire to move.

It is an interesting exercise to step back and examine the process I enter when I write, to document what other artists have said, and to note where artistic endeavours share similar characteristics. The process I have come to trust when writing a book also instructs the way I live my life.

I was raised believing that difficulties belonged to other people. Problems, I was told, were problems: unwanted and undesirable situations that needed to be disposed of quickly, like smelly rubbish. I also assumed that they obeyed logic. Someone gave you a rule, you applied it, and the world was restored.

Both life and writing have shown me that such an approach can be a problem in itself. There are some bothersome things one might be able to excise quickly, then throw out with the one hand while staunching the bleeding with the other. But many dilemmas require patience, and the humility of not knowing the immediate solution, nor what is going to happen next.

There are two distinct methods of writing. In goal-oriented writing, the author knows where and how the story will develop before they have written much at all. They plot out the entire novel before writing it. Many good writers manage to pull off the goal-oriented approach, but it mystifies me. I relate to what I think of as process-oriented writing – starting with an idea and then tracking where it wants to go as a kind of conversation between what I know about the story and what I don't. This method means that I cannot predict the ending of a story before I get there. Events arrive along the way that keep modifying the script, veering it off in directions I had not intended, taking me and the story with it. Even with this work of non-fiction, I am not yet sure how to end it. As in life, endings can be difficult.

Yet living and writing in a process way, I can comfort the part of me that gets anxious about not knowing what is going to happen. Beginning a creative project is an act of faith. From experience, I know that something will turn up to finish it off.

***

The rules of colour theory or musical scales are important tools for the artist to acquire. The study of art history with its canons in painting and dance, music, drama and literature is also valuable. These considerations will naturally inform the artist's work. But there are other tools we cannot learn from textbooks. As an artist, I might have many good ideas, but I have learnt that the muse or the unconscious will often have better ones. If I keep elbowing unbidden images, sounds and events aside, I will not do my best work.

Harold Pinter revealed[96] that two of his plays initiated themselves in his imagination as a spoken sentence. One was 'Where have you put the scissors?' and the other was only one word: 'Dark.' – a response to a question. Many a writer would have dismissed these leads, but Pinter trusted them and ran with them. His job as author was to find out who had said these words and why, and what the ensuing story was all about.

An image arrived in John Fowles' mind of a woman in nineteenth century attire standing on a cliff and looking out to sea. In his collection of essays, *Wormholes*,[97] Fowles notes that he did not know who she was, and what she was doing. He wrote a best-selling book to find that out: *The French Lieutenant's Woman*.

Matisse described the movement of his pencil on the paper as 'the gesture of a man finding his way in the dark'. If the unconscious is able to steer us through areas that our conscious control and intent are blind to in order to shape a coherent and truthful piece, we need to find out how to facilitate this facilitator, rather than obstruct it.

Intuition, or the guiding feelings of yes or no might go against convention, or even break established rules. Going with

DAWN GARISCH

the creative flow might well feel as though you are a pioneer in unfamiliar territory. Following a hunch might lead to a mess; at other times it will enhance the project beyond measure. It can, if truly inspired, even lead to a new way of working and of seeing. An exhibition of African masks influenced Picasso in his work 'Les Demoiselles D'Avignon', a painting that was initially ridiculed, and is now recognised as a ground-breaking artwork, presenting, in the original way it does, desire and fear, servitude and assertion.

The writer, Alvarez, proposes that all true art is subversive, and not only of literary clichés and social conventions. He says 'it also subverts the clichés and conventions you yourself would like to believe in. Like dreams, it talks for parts of yourself you are not fully aware of and may not much like.'[98]

It is important to differentiate whether the inkling of intuition is leading us astray or putting us back on our own track. We all know how that little voice that we take for good advice can completely derail us. If intuition is to be helpful, we need to develop it to make it a reliable tool.

Experience – checking in with reality – can lead to more reliable guidance from our emotions. The need to accumulate experience means we are unlikely to be brilliant artists first off, and not only in the area of technical skills. We have to grow our unique style and voice. Alvarez suggests that in order to grow our creative lives, we also have to grow up: 'By comparing writing and psychoanalysis, I'm implying that finding your own voice as a writer is in some ways like the tricky business of becoming an adult.'[99]

Yet, over and above the learnt, cultivated, mature, independent response that feeds subliminally into what we think of as intuition, there stands the muse, waiting for us to pick up the pen, paintbrush or instrument. The next chapter looks at ways in which we can tune in to her. These tools can help us become better artists, and also become better participants in life as well.

23. Sharpening the Tools

Our real illiteracy is our inability to create.

Friedensreich Hundertwasser, artist and architect

Other than my school experience, I have had minimal formal education in literature, poetry or creative writing. I regret the consequent gaps in my knowledge regarding seminal works and critical thought. Friends of mine who have had tertiary education in this field were taught the useful skill of literary criticism to assess the structure and value of a work. Paradoxically, this has often interfered with their ability to write. When they attempt to express themselves creatively, dissection and analysis kick in prematurely, and the project seizes up. This can even be a problem with people who have been strictly schooled in spelling and grammar.

English Professor, Sondra Perl[100] has looked at how creative writing students apply themselves to the page. She has shown that those who constantly check their work while writing produce prose of a poor standard. They are constantly interrupting the flow of material by proofreading and correcting as they go.

The first recommendation, then, if we are to break through from the rational, ordered, ego-controlled world into that inhabited by the muse, is that we need to abandon all ideas about good syntax and spelling, even our notions of good writing. We must allow ourselves to be carried forward by the writing itself.

I experience this 'breaking through' as moving from writing outside to inside the piece, similar to what happens when I read a book or see a movie. The ones that work dissolve me into their own substance, and I enter the dream. Afterwards, I can step back and analyse my experience, but at the time I must be engaged to the point of losing myself.

Another way to loosen the grip of the ego at the creative edge is to be awake to subliminal clues. This assumes that the unconscious is providing information. Jung's analogy of the relationship between the ego and the unconscious – that the ego is like a cork on the ocean – is an apt one, in that it illustrates the small and limited perspective of the ego in the face of the power and scope of the psyche. It is also an image of the ego's resilience which always returns to the surface after a huge storm. What it fails to portray are the ways in which these seemingly disparate entities are able to communicate.

In workshops, the image I use to illustrate the relationship between the ego and the unconscious is one of a plot of land. We sign the papers, and then set ourselves up, thinking that we own it and it is ours to use as we like. We build a fence which defines the boundary of the plot, and we think of everything inside as belonging to us, and everything outside as foreign, alien, not ours. Yet, try as we might, it is not possible to keep the outside out. Seeds, insects and birds come in on the wind, bringing new life, small animals get in through the slats in the fence, burglars get in over it and help themselves, and underneath what looks like solid, stable ground, is a vast, dark river that bubbles up as a wellspring right where we have laid a concrete path.

Either we attempt again to batten down the hatches and patch the fence, or else we pay attention to those things that seek entry. Something is trying to get in via our dreams, accidents, illnesses and other habits and difficulties: something that can release us from too small an idea of who we are and what we can create.

Altering our perceptions about these intrusions and seeing them instead as helpful messengers opens us to what they want to say. We need to notice that they are around, arriving continually.

I am making an analogy between the difficulties of knowing how to proceed in one's life, as in one's writing. It assumes that the muse in writing, or daimon in life, knows better than we do where we are heading. When the Yoruba 'remember' their lives by 'trying to attune/attain/atone memory and destiny', they are constantly looking for charged clues in their inner and outer environments that link their recall of the past with that which calls to them from the future. They use these associations to assess how well they are tracking their own unique path.

Every day we are bombarded by stimuli, but only a few hold enough power to make it through to memory. These stand like cairns, drawing our focus, glowing in an otherwise grey landscape. These memories not only reveal patterns in our past, but also flag a way forward, in that they contain the motif of our lives. We are called to pay attention to and to develop these themes, even when initially there appears no reason to do so.

In high school I played the part of Prospero in Shakespeare's play *The Tempest*, which is set on an island. Years later, my son was in *The Tempest* twice at different schools – the second time as Prospero. I therefore came to know the play very well. Watching it for the umpteenth time as an adult, some of the core preoccupations of the play spoke directly to my life at that time. Soon thereafter, on the ship to Antarctica, I heard strange stories about Tristan da Cunha, the most remote island in the world. These cues precipitated me into my seat, where I wrote the opening chapter of *Once, Two Islands*. It started as an idiosyncratic reworking of the Tempest – an island story concerning love, betrayal, revenge, forgiveness, and the use and abuse of power – but then developed its own arc.

***

Marion Milner, in her book *An Experiment in Leisure*,[101] observes that there are two different kinds of paying attention: the hard, bright, searing focus of the spotlight, and the soft, broad, encompassing beam of the searchlight. She equates spotlight attention with an intellectual or masculine way, and searchlight attention with a physical or feminine way. Men and women need both ways to live life fully, but our culture promotes the intellectual way.

Trying it out, I sense a distinct difference between spotlight and searchlight – attending with my mind or my body, seeing through my central or peripheral vision, hearing with my ears or my centre. When I shift my attention from the usual mode of spotlight to that of searchlight, I feel an expansion, not only in my mind, but in my body. It is a more inclusive, less hurried and less judgemental way of attending to my life, and it expands the attention I bring to my writing.

Paying attention also means that any occasion becomes an opportunity for the artist. The word opportunity comes from the Latin *porta* meaning entrance or passage through. The portals into the creative space are all around, but I will not notice them if I am focused on the ossified and surface world. Engaging the inner artist makes me more observant, more curious about the situations I unexpectedly get into. Difficulty can be a door into another place that can show me something. It is good training.

I am being one-sided here; difficulty and tragedy are also exactly what they are. It would be wrong to jolly up disaster. But I do remember a shift in my perception that helped me come to terms with the possibility of losing my vision. I realised that I would then discover things about myself and the world that I will not if I remain sighted for the rest of my life.

A while back, I found myself in a long queue at Home Affairs. The non-artist in me objected – I have better things to do with my time! – but the writer I am had an opportunity to observe a slice of life and eavesdrop on conversations. There was a story in each face, there was the drama of the queue. How would one describe the young woman who snapped at her small daughter, or the old man who looked as though he was in pain? How did they get to be who they are? Where are they going?

Or I might find myself trapped at a dinner table next to someone I cannot stand. It can either ruin my evening, or I can switch into writer mode and take mental notes. Next to me is someone who might fuel the beginnings of a memorable character.

I was in a hurry one day when I went into a shop. The man behind the counter was on the telephone, chatting. He indicated that he would be with me in a moment. As the moment dragged into many minutes, I found myself feeling annoyed by his rudeness, and wanting to leave and go elsewhere, but there was something about his tone of voice that kept me there. When he finally put the receiver down, he raised his hands in exasperation. 'I can't believe people!' he exclaimed. 'That was my best friend, who is beside herself because she has just discovered that her fiancé has a child from another relationship and he never told her. I had to point out to her that she is R200 000 in debt, and she hasn't told him!'

That's a loose thread, a fabulous situation with characters that can be followed all the way to a satisfying conclusion. As a writer, I am forever learning about human beings, settings and dialogue. As I pay attention, the hard breathing and rushed pulse of annoyance slows down, and helps to prevent stomach ulcers and high blood pressure.

Being observant requires me to slow down, and to use my senses; I begin to notice images that excite me. Yet if I search for a specific image with spotlight attention, my peripheral vision shuts down. I cannot see properly because I am only looking for the thing I think I need. Many creative moments arise when I am not looking for anything in particular; I am merely being vigilant in a general searchlight way. Unexpectedly, life throws something in my path, and I instantly recognise its charge. I take it home, and begin.

The ego thinks it always knows what's best, but a mechanistic, reductionist view of how the world works is too limited. Now happenstance is again firmly part of the agenda. During the past one and a half centuries, artists and scientists have been entertaining the possibilities and consequences of chance. Darwin in biology, Bohr in quantum mechanics, Freud and Jung in psychology, Tzara in Dadaism and Breton in Surrealism all point to chance as an essential ingredient of life.

Over the millennia, people have ascribed powers of prediction or guidance to specific people, rituals, ancestors or sacred sites. They would travel far to consult an oracle about how to proceed, asking: Should I do this, or that? Should I do it now, or next year? What are the omens and signs?

Today we are split into those who say oracles are superstitious nonsense, and those who claim that approaches such as astrology, psychic readings, God, dreams, the muse, or synchronicity hold the power of the oracle.

The more I pay attention to something beyond my rational understanding, the more assistance I receive in my writing and in life. This is not the frantic seeking of the gold rush. It is a steady focus, a patient gardening. The questions that interest me are rarely answered immediately. A response usually requires waiting for a slow unfolding. It is not a once-off reply, but an ongoing conversation. As a writer I am familiar with minimal cues, small shifts which seem to direct my focus.

***

My script editor used to say that all stories have essentially the same structure: There is a person who has a problem. If the difficulty speaks to our own lives, we want to know what happens next. Writing, I have argued, involves solving not only the tensions on the page, but also the conflicts in myself. The tension can become unbearable. To aid relief, I am sometimes tempted to slip back into control mode, and force a solution. But this cheats both myself and the reader.

The poet Rilke gives this advice to a novice poet: 'Have patience with everything unresolved in your heart and try to love the questions themselves as if they were locked rooms or books written in a very foreign language. Don't search for the answers, which could not be given you now, because you would not be able to live them. And the point is, to live everything. Live the questions now. Perhaps then someday far into the future, you will gradually, without even noticing it, live your way into the answer.'[102]

Living the questions is a radical thought in a culture that is organised around the principle of instant gratification and the belief that the answer to almost anything can be found within minutes on the Internet. Living the questions means developing the capacity to endure not knowing what will happen next, not knowing whether I am right or wrong, nor how long I will have to wait before an answer is revealed to me. Living the questions also requires me to pay attention to the pattern of mysterious partial replies unfolding around me, which can assist me further on the journey of my question, and also indicate whether I am asking the right question in the first place.

Out of a plethora of ongoing goings-on, how are we to decide what is an answer? The oracle, or psyche, does not reveal answers in the way a timetable does.

The feeling function is useful here. By this I do not mean, am I happy or am I sad, but rather: do I value this, what value resides here, does this feel right, or does this feel wrong? Every now and then I write my way into corners that feel terrible, but I persist if they also feel exactly right.

Both the process of life, and that of immersion in writing a novel, feel more and more like patiently living the questions, with no tenaciously-held ending. Where does life call me? What does my soul want of me?

Theodore Roethke, in his wonderful villanelle 'The Waking' suggests that we learn by going where we have to go.[103]

The goal I aspire to while writing or living is to be true to this story, to my story.

***

The musician Sheila Chandra observes that artists are comfortable living with the unknown, as they have had to make a living today out of what didn't exist yesterday.[104]

In order to create, most artists need to be alone, facing the void both within themselves and also within the project. Initially the art work has not yet taken on form, and they are faced with the blankness of the paper or canvas, the emptiness of the stage, or the silence of the air. They must recognise and overcome their fears, otherwise they would never put pen to paper, allow that movement to run through their body, or pick up the flute.

The thing about being alone is that those background voices that we can quieten by keeping ourselves busy with external demands suddenly become very loud, even though they may remain subliminal. If we have crippling critics living in our heads, we will avoid being alone with them. It is therefore essential to transform that undermining enemy into an encouraging helper.

Paradoxically, in the midst of creation, there is that wonderful feeling that one is not alone. The task of gathering together disparate threads into one complete work is an act of connection – with oneself, one's daimon, and with the vast craft of all humankind who over aeons have bent over their looms, easels, drawing pads, cellos, pottery wheels, gardening implements and keyboards, funnelling their efforts and service towards recording and making sense of life.

***

To attend to the minimal cues of the muse, one also has to develop – in fact to long for – what Doris Lessing calls the imaginative space: 'Have you found a space, that empty space, which should surround you when you write? Into that space, which is like a form of listening, of attention, will come the words, the words your characters will speak, ideas – inspiration. If a writer cannot find this space, then poems and stories may be stillborn.'[105]

This is not only a physical place, although it is most concentrated when I am at my desk. It accompanies me wherever I go. It feels like a virtual chamber that floats just behind my right ear, like a thought bubble that contains evolving and dissolving fragments of images, sounds and words. There is always something going on in there, sometimes inaudibly, like a background hum, whether I am lying in the bath or chatting to a friend.

However, my awareness as I go about the ordinary business of life will get me nowhere if I do not bring that attention to the page, canvas or studio. Creating the space and time to sit alone and hazard the first mark, note or movement, is like jumping onto a stepping stone when it is not immediately obvious where the next one is situated. Discovering where to step after the initial jump cannot be worked out in my head. The thing that wants to emerge only becomes apparent in a piecemeal way through repeated acts of applying myself to the work – starting somewhere, and trusting that there is something bigger than I am who is present and ready to supply the other half of the conversation.

The creative process can work immediately, like an instant download, but usually it takes time. I must remind myself to take the long view. Rilke suggests: 'Being an artist means: not numbering and counting, but ripening like a tree, which doesn't force its sap, and stands confidently in the storms of spring, not afraid that afterwards summer may not come. It does come. But it comes only to those who are patient, who are there as if eternity lay before them, so unconcernedly silent and vast. I learn it every day of my life, learn it with pain I am grateful for: patience is everything!'[106]

***

PART
FOUR

Heal Thyself

24. Non-Medicinal Ways to Loosen Torment

Endgame

With modern medicine
doctors can now find
something wrong with everyone.
While shamans and new age healers
can cure anything you haven't got.

Gus Ferguson[107]

My friend and colleague tells her patients it is not in anyone's power to heal another. She says healing is an inside job. All a doctor can do is offer some pointers and medication to facilitate the body's innate capacity to heal itself. Our bodies need our co-operation to do this.

Even the term healing needs revisiting. At a recent psychiatry update for general practitioners, I was pleasantly surprised to find these specialist colleagues recommending that we abandon the idea of cure, and instead encourage our patients to learn to manage their conditions. This, I believe, is true of any chronic malaise, including anxiety. Health is not necessarily synonymous with cure.

Human beings are hard-wired for anxiety, and we have a tendency to get our wires crossed. Fear can either save or ruin our lives. Panic can be paralysing. When Valium was discovered and marketed in the 1960s, it was a remarkably effective treatment for this pernicious condition. But Valium and other benzodiazepines are not recommended for long-term use because they lead to tolerance and dependence. Antidepressants are safer and more effective in treating chronic anxiety.

Popping a pill can banish symptoms, but what of the underlying causes, and how might we address them? Heal thyself is not an injunction to refuse help. Help comes in many forms, and there is plenty of it. This section suggests ways to manage better the authentic insecurities of life. We might thereby loosen our torment without either resorting to medication, or relying on medication alone.

***

At the height of my midlife crisis, the feeling in my body was terrible. The word that came to mind was judder. My edges felt torn and blurred. I had a few incidents where the world felt as though it was turning. Once, while driving, I had to pull over to the side of the road.

Anxiety can be free-floating, formless, expansive. It is hard to deal with because it is so nebulous. It can cause us to act reflexively in an attempt to find relief – a knee-jerk reaction called 'acting out', such as drinking, drugging, compulsive sex, shopping or eating excessively, bullying, or biting nails.

A more helpful response to either acute or low-grade chronic anxiety is to find a container to give the feeling shape and dimension – thus making it manageable. This tendency to return to the container in times of anxiety is evident in small children. They embark perilously from their mother's laps and toddle a metre or two out into the world, only to be seized by apprehension. They come stumbling back into her arms, looking for reassurance.

When we feel alone and unsupported, we turn to substitutes to make us feel better. We all need a container that simulates mother, father, guardian or tribe. We might act confidently in the world, strapping ourselves independently into our own skins, but most of us need to feel that we belong and are held.

When my life was falling apart and the world was turning, I instinctively sought containment by going back into therapy, writing everything down including my dreams, writing poems and lying on the ground. I was so depressed and anxious at that time, I could not work. Fortunately, I had the means to stop working for three months while I got myself back. For much of those three months, I lay curled up in a blanket on the ground in the garden.

Many of our preoccupations are attempts to construct a container against the void. A love relationship, religion, work, a home and sport are all valuable means to reduce anxiety. Creative projects also have the ability to hold us. They supply something of what we need to get our heart rates and adrenalin levels down, to make us pause before reacting, and to slow and deepen our breathing. If we can identify the symbols and images arising out of our distress, and then approach these images through writing, dance, clay, paint or music, we can expand our apprehension of the difficulty. Creative engagement helps us to bear what seems unbearable, and can act as a bridge towards resolving tension.

***

A psychiatrist friend pointed out to me that the image of the mother as a container can be anathema to those who have had a negative mother experience. Paul Ashton has written extensively on creativity and the void.[108] He suggests that creative activities, by connecting us to the unconscious, allow us to understand that we are more like a constellation than a singularity, and as a result we feel less alone. Creativity becomes a view from another star, in other words from points other than the ego. That, he argues, is why it feels like it comes from elsewhere rather than from 'what I know' which is the ego position.

I am reminded that the image that is helpful to me might not be so for another. It is necessary to find the particular and personal images that speak to the motif of each individual's life.

***

Symbol formation is an act of imagination. In their book *The First Idea*, the child psychiatrist Stanley Greenspan and the philosopher Stuart Shanker argue that creating a meaningful symbol requires two things. It can only occur in the context of emotional life. And it only appears when perception is separated from its action.[109] This last attribute allows someone to talk about how he is feeling or to draw a picture of it without having to act on it out in the world.

They show how cultural knowledge passed down through generations is a spur for a baby's brain development, parallel to and independent of genetically-transferred information. The stimuli of care and attention, as well as the teaching of practical skills and language by the tribe, allow for development of new brain circuitry not encoded in DNA. Importantly, these activities also allow for the child to develop the capacity for symbol formation, adequate attention span and reflective thinking. They illustrate how these essential assets are fragile, and how their development can be disrupted by neglect or absent caregivers in early life.

People who have not learnt how to mediate catastrophic emotions such as rage and fear, had their emotional development disrupted in childhood. They are unable to insert a pause between perception and reaction. A pause in that moment gives us an opportunity to weigh up whether our perceptions were perhaps erroneous, whether our emotional reaction is appropriate and what might be going on for the other person(s) involved. It allows us to apply feeling and thinking, recall and knowledge, to try out options in the virtual workspace of the brain, and thereby come to a decision as to which of many different responses is the best one to choose in the circumstances.

Greenspan and Shanker propose that this capacity for the pause originates out of the earliest emotional interactions between infant and caregiver. A baby learns incrementally to read the nuances of another person's facial expression, gesture and tone of voice, and also discovers how she can influence her environment with her own display through movement and sound. The interest and containment of an adequate carer allows the faceted nature of relationship to emerge, whereby the growing child develops the ability to restrain impulsive actions in favour of pausing in order to better 'read' all the signals in an interaction, or non-verbal conversation. This 'reading and reflecting in the pause' relies on symbol formation. In order to think about a person or a happening, the child must create something that represents the real within the virtual workspace of the mind.

Greenspan and Shanker state that when we learn at this early age to transform emotions into long chains of interactive signals, we form an image that's less tied to action, and which can therefore engender meaning and become a symbol. Furthermore, their research suggests that we use such images to plan, solve problems and think.[110]

This important faculty cannot develop without a concerned and attentive care-giving environment that enables the baby to learn back-and-forth emotional signalling between baby and caregiver.[111] Yet even if we have had the good fortune of involved, available and caring parents or guardians, most of us have developed bad habits. Most of us have some area in our lives where we struggle with impulse control, and where our recurrent behaviour gets us into difficulties.

The capacity for symbolic life inserts a considered voice between the obsession of the mind and the compulsion of the body – revved and in tandem – in order to alter the unconscious agreement.

If the body-mind tandem continues to mutter and react unconsciously and repetitively, it limits the whole show to the familiar. I perceive this and I do that. Inserting a pause will also insert anxiety while we search for a new way of responding. In Chapter 35 we will consider how to develop the capacity to resist our habitual modes, and to manage the attendant anxiety.

***

Ken Robinson[112] claims our task in life is to find that space where what we are good at, and what we want to do more than anything, come together. He calls it the Element. Others call it being in the zone. In that space, we feel alive. We feel guided and supported. We do our best work in this place, and we do it with enthusiasm. Ideas and assistance arrive spontaneously. Even though we might be working very hard, it doesn't feel like work. We wake up in the morning looking forward to getting back to it.

This is not to say that living a creative life is easy or pain-free. But it roots us in the feeling of containment, connection and guidance. It is one of the best non-medicinal anxiolytics I know.

Taking free-floating anxiety and doing the work of turning it into an art piece by committing it to paper as a painting or a poem, or finding its shape on the dance floor, or singing it out in the car, not only makes the feeling manageable, but also gives it form out in the world. Outrage, desire, joy, fear and shame need expression, and the stage and the page are places we can go to in order to contain the energy of these emotions and to distil insight and value from our efforts.

***

25. Dealing with the Inner Critic and the Daimon

But I
    subdued
        myself,
            setting my heel
on the throat
        of my own song.

Mayakovsky[113]

The inner critic is one reason many of us are so anxious. The internalised fault-finder is a big factor in why we stop ourselves from doing what we love most, or even from discovering what it is we love to do. Sometimes we don't even realise we have this background niggler.

Most of us are hounded by inner critics for most of our lives – that bullying voice that tells you that you are not good enough. The trouble is, sometimes this feedback is true. Unfortunately, the inner critic does not distinguish between what we do well and what we don't, and secondly, she is often rude and undermining, rather than encouraging.

Inner criticism is not only related to our personal experience, but also to the dictates of the time. Virginia Woolf, in her essay 'Killing the Angel in the House', refers to the difficulties women experienced in her era. To be able to write, she says, women need to kill the angel of the house – meaning they need to say a firm No to the internalised dictum to put other people first, to be pure, and to pretend to be less intelligent than they are.[114]

Killing the critic is an option. But if we try to get rid of something so ingrained, it could come raging back to cause more havoc. Besides, the critic has an essential function. We all need feedback as to how we are doing, but not in a false, undermining way. Feedback can be hard, but we should not dispense with criticism altogether. The question is how to transform the envious destroyer into a helper who delivers criticism in a considered and related way.

We need to allocate an appropriate time and place for criticism. If the critic enters too soon after I embark on a creative project, she might interfere at a stage where my ideas are too sensitive, or too unformed, and ruin the whole endeavour. Ask the critic to wait outside, and invite her in when there is something to show her. Be firm, but kind. The inner critic is as afraid of rejection as we are.

The critic is the appraisal and editing function, the one who can step back and evaluate whether the project is working as a whole, and where it needs further work. Practically speaking, the critic slips in and out all the time, but the more I exercise my creativity in the face of disapproval, the stronger I feel in relation to this entity. The relationship evolves into a partnership where I am better able to argue my case, as well as to consider or assimilate opinions different from those held by my ego without either being defensive, or crumbling.

Teaching the inner critic to be human and humane in relation to a creative enterprise, can have a positive spin-off in the rest of life, where we also undermine ourselves. We need to transform the old habit of acting in our own worst interests into encouraging our best efforts, and acting with kindness and care regarding how we spend our time and energy. If we do not put ourselves first – if we do not care for and about ourselves – we cannot authentically care for and about anyone else either.

The critic is intimately bound up with the ego. Our egos overlap with identity. We need to have form and shape in the world – that fence around the plot of who we are – in order to function and be effective. We need sufficient ego strength to be able to get to work on time, or to stretch up a canvas.

But the ego is too restrictive, too defended. It tends to aim for external goals for a sense of wellbeing, such as control, perfectionism, status, fame and fortune. When we fall short, which is inevitable, the ego brings in its buddy, the inner bully, to tell us we are not good enough and never will be.

Psyche, however, is not interested in the concerns of the ego. Psyche is involved in story and symbol, and we all know that a good story needs highs and lows. Psyche's ally is the daimon, guiding us through the swamps and plateaus of the creative story of our lives.

Paradoxically, paying attention to the demands of the daimon, or muse, does not solve the problem of self-care entirely. Creative urges can become all demanding, all consuming. The daimon wants attention, and she wants it immediately. She has the ability to do just about anything, but we are human. There are many artists who, in service to their craft, have burnt out, or drunk or drugged themselves to illness or death. As we need to humanise the internalised critic in order to live creatively, we also need to negotiate with the forceful, urgent nature of the daimon, and remind her that we have needs and limitations associated with staying alive. Unlike the muse, I need to eat, sleep and walk up the mountain. I need to go to the toilet, or chat with a friend. I need to potter about in my garden, and even sit and do nothing for a while. The daimon, however, rides on my shoulder, commanding, wheedling: Get back to your desk! Pay attention, or the gifts I am showering down on you will be lost! Just one more hour, just another. And another. It doesn't matter that it's three in the morning and that your back is aching. You are tracking treasure, keep going.

Finding a track to follow, nose to the ground, making something out of nothing and keeping company with the charged dance is exhilarating. It is obsessive, a drug. I want more, and more, just a little more. Like a drug, the creative fire can burn one out and ruin one's health. It can, literally, lead to taking drugs to keep one going.

***

At the moment, I feel electric, heightened, floating on top of my lovely life. For the past year, since starting this book, I have felt the gigantic pressure of wanting to drop everything else and sit down and write the whole book immediately. Right now. That is how it feels. Of course, that notion is crazy in that there has been an enormous amount of reading, research, talking things through and processing to develop the content and shape of the project. But my daimon knew exactly what he wanted, and he wanted it *now*. So for a year I have had to resist this continual pressure to get back to the desk, and the accompanying terror that I will forget whatever it was that I, or the book, was on about.

So, to my daimon: thank you for a great morning. Right now, despite your protests, I am going to shut down my laptop. I will have a shower, then go off with some friends to an art gallery, for lunch and a walk.

***

26. Of Creativity, Connections and Healing

Philip Larkin said that a poem is a knife and
fork partnership. The fork identifies an emotion:
spears it, lands it on the poem's plate. The knife
is analytical and technical, wants to 'sort out the
emotion, chop it up, arrange it and say either
thank you or sod the universe for it.' The fork is
what makes readers reach for poetry in a crisis.

Ruth Padel[115]

As I drove to work today, knowing that the complimentary copies of *Trespass* had been delivered to reception and that I would soon have the fruit of a couple of years of inner and outer work in my hand, I pondered the twists and inversions of the psyche. Trespass was not an easy book to write. It is in the form of a journal by a woman utterly different from me, yet who I might have been if I had been born into a different political and social time, and into different family dynamics and circumstances. I wrote my way into her character, and all the way back into boarding school.

One of the difficult things about my experience of boarding school was that there was no privacy. My bed was in a shared dorm, and my access to my own small space, such as it was, was strictly controlled and limited. The authorities even tried to penetrate our minds. The head mistress of one school 'caught' me with money I was going to use to buy a book for a friend for his birthday, and forced me to tell her what I was doing with it.

She called me into her study the following Sunday afternoon to tell me that the book was rubbish, written by a drug addict, and what was I doing reading such a book? She had gone out and bought and read it. It was Bob Dylan's *Tarantula*.

The feeling of invasion and violation from eight institutional years during childhood and adolescence remains with me. Without it I could not have written *Trespass*. I have used my experience and that of others who went to boarding school to construct a fiction that contains a truth, and in doing so, I have a work in the public domain that invites readers into a private world. Reading Phyllis Wilds' personal journal is a trespass and a violation.

My acts of creativity are acts of mental health. I am aware of the irony that, in order to remedy my sense of violation of privacy and integrity at boarding school, I write books which, once out in the public domain, will result in criticism both for and against the text. Critics and readers might well decide a book of mine is rubbish. A published work has a life of its own, and will be seen and interpreted by anyone who reads it through their own experience of the world, as well as being compared with other texts. When I write or create, I drop the barriers erected in defence of my privacy. For the work to be seen, the creator must risk something of herself, otherwise she is writing to a formula. Unlike in childhood, this time I choose to do it. Perhaps that is what heals.

***

Trauma causes a split between the emotional and cognitive centres of the brain, disrupting the ability for meaning making or linear narrative. It leaves the brain at the mercy of powerful, distressing images and emotions. It's like a short circuit – normal connection between the two parts is damaged in some way.

Poetry engages with emotions, the felt-sense of
the body, images, metaphors and searches for
a language thereby making a connection to the
meaning making centres of the brain. It acts as a
channel or bridge between them.

Poetry like trauma has a deep connection with
the body and the senses, but it also connects
with the conscious mind as it grapples with
language. So we could see poetry as providing
the bridge between implicit and explicit memory
in order to provide the vital connection necessary
for recovery.

Seni Senivaratne[116]

We know from real-time scans of the brain that, when confronted
by metaphor – the basic tool of poetry – more areas light up
than during any other activity.[117] Metaphor and symbol arise
from association, and the majority of our brain tissue is devoted
to associative tasks of meaning-making. These brain areas link
up *this* with *that* so that we can make sense of the world and
ourselves as we receive information from the inner and outer
environments. Writing poetry stimulates the connections for
meaning-making, and thereby helps trauma survivors integrate
the horror of their experience and move on with their lives.

With this finding in mind, the psychoanalyst Margaret
Wilkinson proposed in a lecture I attended in Cape Town that
therapists should perhaps make more use of metaphor when
working with patients. She says that those patients whose
connections within the occipito-frontal cortex did not develop
well due to early childhood trauma might be helped through
mobilising connections using symbol.

The *Journal of Poetry Therapy* cites a case study entitled
'Runaway with words: Teaching poetry to at-risk teens'.
Through various exercises, oral recitations and conversations,

troubled teens in Florida's runaway shelters learn basic writing skills that help them gain control over their emotions.[118]

In a pilot study designed to evaluate the use of group poetry therapy interventions with cancer patients there was a significant decrease in suppression of emotions and in anxiety in those who wrote poetry. There was no change in the control group. The study concluded that a poetry therapy intervention may improve emotional resilience and anxiety levels in cancer patients, but recommended larger randomised control group trials to test this further.[119]

***

Words have alternately been described as inadequate to the task of describing emotion, and also as deliverers, providing a means to put what you are feeling into a form that can be transmitted to another. Sometimes when we identify a background unease by naming it, we can access insight and relief.

Words have limitations in that they can only act as an approximation for something else that is not composed of words. Despite this, words are able to connect us back to the images they stand in for – back to the poetic base of the mind.

***

27. Image and Imagination

Those images that yet
Fresh images beget,
That dolphin-torn, that gong-tormented sea.

Yeats[120]

Watching children playing the game that my young sons called 'jubbetend' (just pretend), it is clear they use their versatile imaginations to experiment with ideas and feelings, to practise control over a situation, to expand their talents and social skills, to mimic, learn and just to have fun. The poet Ted Hughes notes that it is this gift of imagination, not the teaching of grammar, that determines the writer,[121] or any artist. Yet he and Ken Robinson[122] express concern that our school systems squash, rather than enhance, this skill.

Mimicking or miming is one way we learn. Imagination allows us to expand beyond our own experience. It also allows us to dream into other lives – how we would feel and respond if we were in someone else's shoes. This function of the frontal lobes imparts the essential social capacity for empathy. Also, imagining a life different from the current one enables someone in trouble to initiate the steps necessary to change. It can increase our complexity, and our repertoire for living.

***

Imagination can heal or harm us, assist or sabotage us.

When we are confronted by a gun-toting robber in our home, or when we are told we have cancer, or when we have to speak in public, or when we are retrenched, we usually visualise the worst possible outcome: death or disability, humiliation or poverty.

My patient who cannot sleep because he is afraid of dying, has an inflexible image of the future. His imagination has frozen into a single image which overrides the reality of his youth and health.

Imagining ourselves as victims has physiological effects. We might have been subjected to the most appalling violence and misfortune, but not allowing any other re-imagining of the event or situation keeps us in a state of chronic stress. Ernest Hartmann,[123] a psychiatrist and laboratory dream researcher, has found that dreams have a healing function in people who have suffered trauma. Dream images can slowly integrate the traumatic event by changing how the trauma is represented. Over time, the event is incorporated into the larger dynamics of dream life. However, in people suffering from Post Traumatic Stress Disorder (PTSD), dream images associated with the trauma congeal into a repetitive stereotype.

Robert Bosnak, a psychologist who works with dreaming states, does not wait for sleep and dreaming in order to engage with patients on modifying and integrating the trauma. He encourages them to induce a flashback of the event, and to describe it in as much detail as possible. The advantage is that, even though imagining a trauma will evoke it as if it was actually happening, his patients are at the same time aware of being in a room with the support of the therapist. In describing in vivid detail what they are seeing and experiencing, from the sensation of the floor, to the colour of the wall or sky, he asks them to note whether anything has changed since the initial event, which it often has. This can help people with PTSD to integrate the experience.[124]

***

Image is psyche.

C. G. Jung[125]

The medical profession sees disease processes as malfunctions in the body that require treatment. We ignore the metaphoric motif. Doctors are trained to interpret symptoms, because we know they are associated with specific diseases. A burning sensation in the epigastrium that the patient reports as feeling like fire is usually a direct pointer to inflammation of the gastric mucosa. This is an elegant and practical approach to diagnosis and treatment, but it can only operate on the level of the fixed image. By treating the symptom with a proton pump inhibitor and altered diet, the symptom subsides, the gastric mucosa returns to normal, and we say that the patient is healed. But the symbol contained in the image of burning – which might lead off in many directions, from the consuming flames of desire to the lava of unspilt rage – is lost. Mindell[126] suggests that this unprocessed, unconscious material shifts from disturbing the body to disturbing another aspect of our humanity, our relationships, for example.

When a woman loses her breast to cancer, her response to the facts and flesh of the matter is likely to be fear and horror, but if she can connect to the myth, symbol and story evoked by the image, it might help her to locate the event in a metaphoric way within the rest of her life's motif, with some relief. The symbol of a woman without breasts is extremely powerful, and not only in a negative way. Myth has it that the Amazon women cut off one of their breasts to aid their use of a bow and arrow, an image which leads to others, and is therefore not fixed and lifeless.

***

Advertisers know how powerfully we respond to images. We are assailed by a multitude of visual cues through television, billboards, mail drops and posters. They all jostle for our attention, using clever ploys.

Advertisements nowadays have little to do with information. Their success lies in how well they can manipulate our attention, our associations and our pockets. The images are carefully chosen to stimulate anxiety or desire – linking our drive to be happy to an object or a way of life. They depict states we are encouraged to strive for, or those we are encouraged to fear – being lonely, uncool, exposed to germs, hungry, injured, dead or old. The image, losing connection with the depth and mystery of the symbolic, evokes a knee-jerk response. Reflexes, like symbols, bypass the analytic brain. But symbols, unlike reflexes, make meaning in the associative cortices.

Commercial images lean heavily on us, trying to influence our behaviour towards handing over money. Dream images challenge us in a completely different way. They often present aspects of ourselves which we find incompatible with who we think we are. James Hollis comments that, as we know we did not consciously create those dream dramas, they remind us that some separate agency of awareness is observing and reporting in.[127]

Dreams have also been called God's most unappreciated gift. Not everyone agrees. Some neuroscientists describe dreams as the attempts of the brain to cobble images together out of the random and excess neuronal discharge created by the lower midbrain as it attends to essential functions while we are asleep.

Yet images arriving through dreams and daydreaming have on occasion assisted scientists and inventors to solve problems. Some famous examples of this include the snake image that gave Kekule the idea for the structure of benzene and Darwin's living tree metaphor for the evolutionary process. Seeing a spear with a hole in the blade while he slept gave Elias Howe the solution for inventing the sewing machine, and James Watson's dream of a spiral staircase helped solve the puzzle of the structure of DNA. These are famous examples, yet we all have dream images that might point towards solutions to the problems that preoccupy us.

Using dream-related tools, Bosnak also assists those wanting to explore illness and creative blocks. A notice announcing his visit to South Africa arrived in my inbox at the time I was struggling with the many quandaries presented by the task of writing this book: finding the tone, form, content and language that would best convey what I wanted to set out on paper. I was feeling restless, distracted; I procrastinated, spending hours on emails and YouTube; I walked, read and pottered, avoiding the next step, waiting for help.

I booked to go on his workshop to find out more about his approach, then made a few private appointments. I explained to him what I was trying to achieve in the book, and the problems I was having. Bosnak encouraged me to sit quietly and become sensorially aware of all the elements of the situation and the associated images. We then worked towards a point where I held these images *simultaneously* in my body, rather than chronologically.

This method acts as a pressure cooker, increasing tension between all aspects of the situation. It is very difficult to juxtapose contradictory emotions, joy, fear and pain, for example, but this is the way of story. All parts must be represented, otherwise there is no completion. Then, out of the tension, the constellation of images begins to change and resolve in ways that are experiential and non-rational, and are therefore always unexpected.

Entering a hypnogogic, or pre-dreaming, state, I saw that inside the darkness of my trunk – trunk, rather than abdomen, is the word that came to mind – there appeared a luminous and thin glass cylinder suspended diagonally, pointing towards my heart. On closer inspection, I noticed that the cylinder was both a wand and a test tube. My serious mood lightened immediately at the playfulness of the unconscious, and I became full of enthusiasm to follow that image of magic, creativity and science wherever it might lead me. I understood: I must bring these disciplines together by writing in a heartfelt way.

Across cultures and religions, throughout the ages, human beings have consulted Psyche – or the gods, wellspring or oracle – using dreams and image. They would usually journey to a sacred place and sleep there, asking for a dream to assist them. Dreams were portents, omens, they were seen as the language of the gods. They were a place one could go for assistance. Dreams were a way of going back to the source or the wellspring of the life force.

***

Imagination is not a single event. It is like finding the end of a piece of twine and following it. By its nature, it is engrossing. Tracking the thread occurs in varied ways in the landscape of a child's imagination: drawing, daydreaming, playing in sand or with an army of sticks or toys, building towers or dams, singing or visiting an imaginary world or person at the top of a tree or under a bed, exploring the contents of a workshop or a sewing room, draping sheets over furniture to create houses or constructing islands with mashed potato and gravy. Entering imagination is to enter another world, and another area of the brain. That immersion is usually why a child at play cannot hear his parent call, not because he is 'naughty'.

Engaging in play at an early age helps the child discover what he wants to become, or, rather, what the daimon wants of him. Learning to follow flow is a skill essential to attending to one's passion and calling, and it is learned young. Yet we frequently interrupt the child at play, pulling their focus towards the practicalities of timetables and the dominance of the 'real'. Imagination requires concentration and absolute attention. It requires others to respect the imagination at work. Play is a child's job.

These observations do not only apply to the realm of childhood. The obsessions and necessities of imagination in creative tasks need our focus. Too often we do not respect the pull of our creativity; frequently we interrupt it by always giving priority to the mundane activities of life and the demands of the modern way.

***

DAWN GARISCH

28. Going to Source

> ...Here, within the slow
> refrain of stone, is water plaited round
> a rock[128]

When my friend Veronica invited me to stay in her rural cottage in Wales, I thought I would much rather visit Mali or Cambodia. The United Kingdom seems too familiar, embedded as it is in my psyche from childhood through fairy tales and marmalade, murderous kings and crown jewels, roses and the Brontés. If I were to travel, I reasoned, I wanted mystery and difference. Going to Britain would feel like going backwards.

But Veronica is also a writer, and we had spent a prolific ten days together in my Cape Town home, bent over our laptops, reading each other's work, encouraging and challenging each other over coffee at the local deli. We are good for each other in the creative domain. At some point, Veronica let slip that she might not be able to keep the Welsh retreat for much longer in addition to her London flat. Then she clinched it by telling me about St Cybi's well.

There are wellsprings situated all over Ireland and Wales that have been attributed with healing properties for centuries. Initially pagan sites, they were annexed by the Catholic church early in the first millennium AD, and each assigned a saint. St Cybi (pronounced, disappointingly, Cubbi) has presided over a well in northern Wales on the Lleyn Peninsula since the sixth century. The sick would travel there as the waters were said to heal many conditions, from blindness to scrofula. Pilgrims on their way to the abbey on Bardsay Island, another holy site off the tip of the peninsula, would also stop over at the well.

It was suddenly clear to me that I would make a pilgrimage to St Cybi's well; a year earlier, I had attended a workshop on 'Returning to the Source' run by the Jungian analyst and author,

Sylvia Perera. She had visited and researched most of the Celtic wellsprings in Ireland, and in the workshop she presented an ancient approach to both healing and consulting the oracle that has been used for millennia. Sylvia illustrated how this approach derives from and refers back to the psyche as helper, or source. She outlined nine steps to this process of how to approach the well, how to ask for and to receive healing or an answer, and how to return to one's life and integrate what one has received.

Few of us make pilgrimages to actual healing wellsprings, but we all turn to places of calm and comfort, and of revelation and encouragement. Dreams, poetry, gardening, prayer, painting, dancing, meditation, singing, making love, and walking in nature are some examples of journeying to source for a sense of connectedness, guidance and healing.

The first step on the ancient path to the wellspring was to set one's intention. The physically sick wished for healing. Those that consulted the oracle wanted advice concerning relationships, work or politics. But the goal is often not conscious as we venture towards source, and as I boarded the plane to Gatwick, I had no special intention.

On my first day in Wales, Veronica took me to St Cybi's well. We approached it through an old metal gate and across a field, through an opening in a mossy stone wall and down a path next to the stream. There was no-one else about, no stalls selling kitschy mementos, no tours, no restaurants. We came to a ruin of an ancient stone building set against dark trees. There were two chambers within its walls, one containing the small bath fed by the spring, and the other containing a large hearth where travellers would rest after drinking from and immersion in the sacred waters, while they waited for healing.

The rain, as we stripped off our clothes, was colder than the water. We dipped and drank, and drank again from the clear, delicious water, and dripped our way back to the car.

That night after supper, sitting around the fire playing Balderdash with Veronica's children and grandchildren, I felt very close to source. It felt as though an unformed and unarticulated question of mine had nevertheless been answered. I was reminded that the psyche reveals itself in images rather than words, and that concerns do not necessarily need to be expressed verbally in order to get a response from the realm of the unconscious.

I am younger than Veronica, and my sons are leaving home. I have been suffering a natural grief concerning a normal loss, yet knowing that has not felt helpful. Welcomed into the circle of Veronica's extended family, I saw her grandchildren turning their beautiful, open faces to her with questions and observations. I witnessed her heartfelt and practical help. Their interaction with her was a moving, living example of the return to source. I felt encouraged and healed.

Life and Psyche keep bubbling up like water from the depths; both day and night they continually offer refreshment and opportunities. All we need do is drink.

***

29. Adequate Images

We comprehend... that nuclear power is a
real danger for mankind, that over-crowding
of the planet is the greatest danger of all. We
have understood that the destruction of the
environment is another enormous danger. But I
truly believe that the lack of adequate imagery is
a danger of the same magnitude. ...What have
we done to our images? What have we done to
our embarrassed landscapes? I have said this
before ... if we do not develop adequate images
we will die out like dinosaurs.

Werner Herzog, film maker[129]

Advertising corrupts the image. Stasis too can do this. Through denial and self-deception, and the refusal to participate creatively in the psyche, we become stuck with stagnant images of ourselves and of the world. As the free flow of information molecules in the body is optimal for health, so also is the free interplay of image.

Perfection is one such fixed and dominant image in our airbrushed culture. When we aim for perfection, we madly split off from all the other aspects of life that end up somewhere else as other people's problems. The methods we use in attempting to achieve the god-like goal of perfection – pesticides, genetic engineering, disposables, experiments on animals, cheap energy, flying in out-of season produce – can become the suffering and problems of others. The convenience and economy of inexpensive clothing and food and our disposable way of life may be directly related to the inconvenience of others working in sweat shops and coal mines or to the suffering of animals in battery farms, or to the hidden costs of people and animals living next to or affected by rubbish dumps and nuclear plants.

Splitting our world into perfection on the one side and waste and ugliness on the other also means that we see excrement as disgusting and germ-filled, rather than as part of the natural round of eating, digesting, excreting and fertilizing. Our urine and faeces are intended to put back into the soil what we have taken from it, so as to feed those plants that have fed and will again feed us. Peasant farmers know this. A friend, while visiting India, saw farmers squatting in their rice paddies in the mornings. Maxine Hong Kingston relates in her book *China Men* how, if a farmer had to defecate while visiting a neighbour, he would take his turd home for his own crops. Excrement was regarded as valuable.

But since we discovered that faeces can be the carrier of serious disease, we have changed our attitude, and are disgusted to the point that we cannot even deal with our children's poo in towelling nappies. Instead we throw their excrement into the bin for someone else to deal with.

We cannot recognise the good in the bad, nor the bad in what we consider to be good. We become more and more distanced from the eternal cycle of the ways of the world and of nature.

***

The traditional Native American way recommends that, before we commit to a course of action, we should consider the consequences seven generations hence. If our culture took that seriously, we would have to slow down. We would consider and reconsider, rather than rushing ahead on the adrenalin of instant gratification and immediate results. It would also result in extreme conservativism, and would obstruct much innovation and spontaneity.

If we stopped to examine our actions, we would have to consider that for every gain there is a loss, and for every loss there is a gain. Everything that stands tall in the light of innovation and discovery throws down a long shadow. In the documentary *Corporation* (2003), a business magnate who runs a carpet making empire comes across a book that sets out how human progress is destroying the planet. Instead of engaging the default mode of defensiveness, denial and shifting the blame, he takes this on. His factories are being redesigned towards natural solutions, and he has become a motivational speaker at business conferences. He tells his colleagues that business entrepreneurs, like himself, regard themselves as 'the captains of industry', but they are, in fact, the 'plunderers of the earth'.

Over the years I have attended to many patients who have been in motor vehicle accidents. Not one has ever told me that they caused it. It seems that it is extremely difficult for human beings to admit responsibility for their actions. This is in part a problem of imagination. We are, on the whole, invested in an image of who we are which may well be way off the mark.

***

One way of getting to know ourselves better is through the imaginative, creative act. I find it liberating to put myself in the shoes of someone I think of as being different to me. Through writing, dance, drawing, voice work, or even music, I can imagine my way into how it feels to be absolutely anything – selfish, furious, gentle, beautiful, disabled, animal, murderous, dead, a different gender or nationality, or old. The playwright, Sam Shepard says he loves that writing gives him the ability to be a woman, or a child.

Creative exploration loosens us up out of our habitual ways of experiencing the world. A creative project allows us to act out our deepest shadow fantasies and fears in safety, rather than going out to throw bricks through windows, to give someone a bloody nose or to sleep with a stranger, with all the regrets and consequences that follow. It allows expression to the things we have wisely or unwisely repressed, which could otherwise grow into a rabid monster living under the metaphorical stairs. It can cultivate empathy for others, and foster integrity – the capacity to be a congruent person who is in touch with all aspects of her personality. It exercises the neural circuits that have to do with the imaginal.

***

The psychoanalyst Lena Vasileva proposes that the norm is an enemy of the artist, as it destroys the imagination. The norm hides the extremes of light and dark in psychological life. She claims that darkness is a necessary driver for the creative process, and that imperfection and creativity are essential partners. [130]

'Normal' truncates our aesthetic choices. If it is true that the task of life is to develop who we are or who we are meant to be, it requires a switched-on and tuned-in imagination. If I am to develop my character, I must foster an aesthetic which has little to do with the mainstream. How we dress, what objects we live with, the rhythms of our lives, how we spend our time, the food we eat and how we prepare it, what our gardens look like, what animals we live with, how we move and sing, all display character. They are the result of how we engage with life on a continuum from the functional to the decorative. We might decide to live with our grandparent's furniture for most of our lives, or to abandon city life to live in a seaside shack. We might shave our hair off or only wear white cotton.

We all need to develop the main character of our lives, and we need imagination to do it. Story plays an essential part in the development of a child's talent for life. Yet nowadays there is little emphasis on the importance for all children to be exposed to stories from an early age, other than those on television. And television is usually a poor substitute for books. Unlike fairy stories or folk lore, TV emphasises the norm through programme content and invasive advertisements; through its visual nature it supplants much of what would otherwise be imagined by the child (as everyone knows who has seen their childhood story favourites from Alice in Wonderland to Pooh Bear morphed into Disney clones); and it dispenses with the storyteller, the adult or older sibling who reads the book or tells the tale, and who can interact with the child around images and words.

***

Culturally, we have a tendency to see things in relation to their opposites. The binary of good/bad, up/down, in/out, happy/ sad, sick/well, asleep/awake, tense/relaxed, old/young all contain the image of the split. On closer examination, this is usually a false construct. Life is more like a rheostat than a switch. Yet we turn most things into either this or that, setting up a situation where we must cast our lots in with one side or the other and announce the winner, or the correct way of being. Thinking in opposites does not allow for gradation and nuance. It promotes domination, victimisation and control. The binary is anxiety-provoking, turning everything into a this or a that, a right or a wrong, a black or a white. Experiencing life as multiplicity is not only anxiety-relieving, it is also closer to the truth of the way life really operates: as a pale[tte or range].

It would appear that the binary is starting to break down. In academia, the old ways of segregating everything are giving way. The traditional world view of the specialist focusing in on one field is making way for the expert who can read the interconnectedness of life. A marine biologist famous for his work concerning reproduction in the sea urchin is being superseded by those who are researching the interplay of all life forms in the intertidal zones. The science of the singular is being replaced by the ecology of dynamic pluralism.

In behavioural science there is increasing acknowledgement that we are the product of the interplay of complex factors, not only of our genetic expression. Instead of the linear, determinist influence of DNA, Greenspan and Shanker suggest that the old debate of nature versus nurture is a false one. They show that our genetic inheritance and our environment are constantly influencing each other, and they liken this to the way Fred Astaire and Ginger Rogers communicated with each other on the dance floor.[131]

In the field of epigenetics, scientists are researching all factors that influence the development of an organism in addition to DNA. How, when and why a gene expresses itself is a function of the intra- and extracellular environment. There appears to be a conversation going on at this level too.

In the field of neuroimmunology, these shifts are also apparent. I was taught at medical school that the endocrine, nervous and immune systems operated virtually independently of each other. They existed as hierarchies with the brain as top dog. We were taught that neurotransmitters are the substances that convey information across the synaptic gap between nerve endings. Now scientists have found that neurotransmitters exist in many parts of the body, and are often released at quite a distance from the receptor. They exist in large concentrations in the gut, and also on cells belonging to the immune system. In fact, neurotransmitters that initiate and control mood in the brain are also secreted by cells in the immune system.[132] Our physiology is co-ordinated by the actions of these discrete and specific messenger or information molecules, or psychoimmunoendocrine network.[133]

The implications of this new way of understanding the functioning of the body are enormous. Firstly, they challenge the dualistic and reductionist model of mind and body as distinct and frequently oppositional entities. They also suggest that our emotions are linked to the flow and functioning of information molecules, and that we need the free flow of emotion as one of the important components of information in the physical system.

It strikes me that ideas about the body seem to reflect the Zeitgeist, or the dominant way systems are described in other disciplines. The Newtonian/Cartesian idea of the world is mechanistic, dualistic and hierarchically determined. A hierarchy implies that orders get handed down from something or someone who oversees, controls and is in charge of the entire operation, whereas a network denotes a system where power and knowledge do not reside in any one part, but are expressed by means of interaction.

Bosnak's approach to working with the psyche by holding disparate images simultaneously in the body also operates on the level of the network. Information from all parts of the system – even contradictory notions – needs to be present for new knowledge to arise.

In a network, as opposed to a hierarchy, there might well be connections that do not operate according to cause and effect. This would allow for synchronicity. Networks might permit paradox and contradiction to co-exist without cancelling each other out, revealing a multifaceted view of reality.

Another fallen image from my medical school days is how a drug works at cellular level. We were taught that a drug activated a receptor on a cell rather like a key fitting into a lock. Candace Pert has shown that this stiff, mechanistic analogy is incorrect, and that information molecules and drugs act on the receptor through vibrations.[134]

The images held by our society and by scientists about the way things work are under review. Perhaps we need to review our own images as well.

***

Journalists keep us up to date with current news, and our culture pays attention to what they report. Artists are also reporting back, but they reflect on the Zeitgeist – the themes, symbols and motifs of our time. Yet most of us do not make the effort to connect with the important ideas they impart. If we do, we often whizz through a gallery in our lunch hour, and say that we saw the exhibition.

The poet and writer, Ruth Padel, compares poetry to a tiny and stubborn David standing up to the violent Goliath of injustice and repression. She points out that one of the first things tyrannical regimes do is to ban poems and literature, and imprison poets and writers.[135]

Art is fertilizing. Being alert to what artists are saying and thinking through engaging with verbal, visual, and sound symbols can help stimulate our own creativity, and can wake us up to what is going on in our world.

***

Desire is a motive force, and heroes are propelled by necessity. When one withholds a toy the child wants, making him wait for his birthday, the child has time to experience an amplification of what he so desperately desires, and thereby to form an imaginal relationship with it. As Hyde suggests, consciousness awakes when we manage to restrain our appetites and develop mastery over our impulses.[136]

Desire is on a continuum with libido, love, sexuality and creativity. They are all motivating and charged forces that seek connection. They do not have much to do with logic, nor with choice. One does not choose to be drawn to a person, a painting, or a way of life. Desire has a trajectory, it shows us the way forward. Like envy, it informs us as to what we want. We imagine into that which we don't yet have, and develop ideas of how to get it.

The choices in the face of desire are to step towards it, to observe it without acting on it, or to turn away. But there is nothing we can do about the calling itself. If we respond to the call, we find ourselves drawn on still further. The seeking that emanates from the psyche, or the muse, is not the same as wanting a BMW sports car; once you have it, you have it. Nor is it like the cyclical obsessive-compulsive craving of addiction that can never be quenched – one is too many, a thousand is never enough.

Setting out on the imaginal journey of a creative task, which leads simultaneously out into the world and inward towards yourself, is like following a Braille trail. You cannot see where you are going, and you can only imagine beyond the point you have attained. Reaching each stepping stone satisfies desire sufficiently to encourage the curiosity and drive required to continue to the next one.

**

30. Image and the Body

Appointment[137]

The waiting room contains several people,
waiting. Those who can read flip through
magazines; others stare at the wall inside their
faces, their white sticks tucked at their sides.
They come, like me, waiting in their skins, waiting
for hope, cure and light.

The world is fading.
Inside my eye I embark
on a trampoline parabola,
grappling weightlessness against gravity.
Up here, I can see beyond the wall, I can see
through catches in conversation, past
the incomplete gesture, I catch
the bat-flit across a face. I look
for an answer.

The receptionist calls. I stare bereft at the
ophthalmologist's stab of light, consumed by
the need to puncture night. He leans back, head
erased by blur. On the wall behind him hangs a
box of lit letters that have nothing to do with love
or story.

After-images bloom in darkness;
film burns open, fades to black
thumbs press prints down hard
inside my tired eyes.

The doctor says, sincerely: The important
difference is between dark and light.

Images fall through holes,
through blanks in absence.

I leave clutching another important appointment.
I can barely see through tears as I walk away,
fettered by images of flight.

This is what doctors have to say about my condition: it is an autoimmune disorder that affects my connective tissues. Medical science has not yet been able to discover the cause of this, nor of other related diseases, including systemic lupus erythematosis, rheumatoid arthritis, ulcerative colitis, Crohn's disease and ankylosing spondilitis.

In my case, the connective tissues of the joints of my spine and the membrane over the muscles in my back are affected. The illness has also appeared on and off in my right shoulder joint and my Achilles tendons. It used to flare in the pigmented layer in the back of my eyes, and has left me with damaged vision.

Evidence-based medicine deals with the objective body, which can be measured, dissected, looked at under the microscope and subjected to chemical and radiological tests. It can be acted on by medical chemicals or operated on to excise, incise, and to otherwise fix what is broken or faulty. The objective body can also be compared to other bodies to see whether and how it has strayed from the norm. Mainstream medicine describes illness and injury from a perspective outside the body under deliberation.

Many complementary and psychological therapies focus on the subjective body – the precise and sensory way we experience our symptoms. Process work, embodied imagination and my friend Dea's process approach to homeopathy, to name a few, have encouraged me to pay attention to the images or symbols that arise out of my experience of the illness. This has helped me to get to know myself better and to decrease my stress levels.

When trying to describe physical sensations and disabilities, patients must translate diffuse and nebulous visceral, visual, sound and movement information arising from the body into words. This can be difficult, although people usually become energised when attempting this. Patients will spontaneously offer similes and metaphors when they describe symptoms: 'it is as though someone is sitting on my chest', or 'it sounds as though a mosquito is stuck in my ear', or 'the feeling in my back is like ice dropping down it'. One six-year-old boy told me that his cough is like a car trying to start in the morning.

We know there is no-one on the chest, no mosquito, no car and no ice. Yet we experience these sensations vividly as though they are actually happening, or as one might feel them in a dream. We tend to dismiss these experiences as quaint imaginings and move swiftly on to proven methods of diagnosis and treatment. However, I have found two approaches to the symbols thrown up by illness that have contributed to my wellbeing.

A psychoanalyst working with cancer patients noted that their subjective experience of illness contained similar images to those appearing in their dreams. Arnold Mindell[138] suggests that we dream continually and that symbolic life passes untrammelled and autonomously from sleeping to waking states. He has developed a methodology to work with dream and body signals by encouraging the participant to deepen attention. He uses the idea of the beginner's mind, or what social anthropologists call 'making strange', by suspending the ego's tendency to interpret based on what it already knows. Mindell suggests that our cultural tendency to dissect, analyse and pronounce upon the meaning of an event, illness or dream is comparable to colonisation. The ego attempts to dominate and control, subjugating any strange or incomprehensible elements to its dictums, and presuming to understand material from the unconscious even though it is foreign in its essence.

Like the early European colonisers, we will never understand the outlandish and exotic inhabitants of the psyche if we rush in to assign meaning to them. Interpretation can shut down observation, and box in experience. Logic and reason have important roles to play, but they are overvalued in the world. They are our default mode and must therefore be purposefully restrained so that other equally valuable forms of intelligence can emerge.

Mindell encourages the person to follow the image of the illness, problem or dream into movement, drawing, sound and voice work. When we amplify or inhibit an unconscious impulse, associations can break through into consciousness.

Bosnak also uses amplification, but he attempts to recreate the dream space as closely as possible. This means sitting quietly and going inward to visit the dream, event or symptom as a flashback. He discourages any acting out of the experience. When we experience the sensation of moving in a dream, we are not moving at all.

***

Keeping open to unconscious information presenting as physical disturbances might be more important than being healed of a chronic, intransigent illness. If the condition resolves as a result of paying attention to symptom motifs, well and good. But focusing on healing can shut down curiosity and override meaning.

Is there a meaning in illness? There are join-the-dot interpretations of disease, for example a heart attack can point directly to poor lifestyle choices. These associations clearly should not be ignored. However, there is strong, albeit anecdotal, evidence that symptoms also contain non-causal meanings which are individual in nature. But how to access them?

Some practitioners have published interpretations of symptoms. For example, Louise Hay correlates symptoms with specific character traits and psychological tendencies. These interpretations might help loosen up the enquirer to consider aspects of herself that she would normally resist. However, there is a problem with didactic association: it strips the image of its power. The cluster of associations is reduced to a one-liner.

When we interpret our illness or dreams, we might be right most of the time, but we will be wrong some of the time. As we won't know whether we are wrong or right in any particular individual, it is imperative rather to keep an open, or beginner's, mind. This strategy is also essential because interpretation is linked to the ego, and the ego might well bring in the critic. It used to be commonplace for disease to be seen as divine punishment, and we are still apt to fall into the blame trap, as cancer survivors well know. Telling someone that his cancer is caused by repressed anger, or that he will get better if he thinks more positively is glib, insulting, and is loading someone who already has too much to bear. Just as we do not reproach ourselves for our nightmares, it is counterproductive to infer that we have brought our physical difficulties upon ourselves because of weaknesses of character.

If we refrain from methods that close down possibilities, and instead train ourselves to stay with the image, we will allow it to reveal itself on its own terms and in its own language. The rational workings of the mind must take a back seat while we process symbolic, poetic manifestations through our senses. This requires us to resist the impulse to rush off into our heads and intellects, and to stay in the moment and in our bodies and with the broad searchlight of perception. No quick cut of the incisive mind can help here, only a patient attending to and tending the kaleidoscope of dream and image evolving.

The damage to my eyes has left me with swirling debris and an incomplete ring of central blindness called a scotoma. This development, worsening on and off over many years, used to leave me feeling panicked at the prospect that my vision might deteriorate to the point of not being able to write, or drive. I was shocked by and resistant to the tragedy that was befalling me. Panic is visceral. It clamped my body. I felt suffused with all the physiological chemistry that goes with grief and dread.

Yet, when a trainee of Mindell's helped me approach the visual disturbances of my disease as symptom-symbol-metaphor, I had a completely different response. I am not a traditionally religious person, but when I concentrated on the scotomas, they appeared one moment as haloes, and the next as the biblical account of the burning bush: the mystery of the bush on fire that nevertheless was not being consumed. I was suffused with awe. I felt held, radiant, and completely at one with what was happening to me. I felt I was standing before a great mystery. Reverence and comfort flooded me as a whole body sensation.

The transformation from fear to a sense of wonder, at-one-ness and acceptance, both derived from exactly the same source, is fascinating to me. My life has been enriched by experiencing illness metaphorically. My eyes have not deteriorated in the past nine years, and my ophthalmologist has encouraged me to consider my eye condition as 'burnt out'. My partially damaged sight and the burning bush image remain, however. The impairment to my vision cannot improve.

The healthy plant that is nevertheless on fire and the fire burning on ice are images that will accompany me until I die.

***

While working with Robert Bosnak, using the technique he calls embodied imagination, I described the pain in my back. It feels as though a dog has gripped the right side of my thoracic back muscles in its teeth. Its jaws are locked. It will never let go. I feel despair. I have lived with this tenacious and obdurate canine for years. Robert got me to focus very clearly on the sensation of the clench in my back, then he asked me to describe what it is like inside the mouth of the dog.

With this switch, it suddenly felt as though I was a tiny embryo, held gently in the pink, warm mouth of a crocodile. It was very safe; womb-like. I could relax in there, knowing that I was contained inside the fierce mother. The image of the clamped dog that I have carried all these years changed into that of a crocodile carrying its young in its mouth in order to protect them.

This is particularly apt as I am dealing with the normal loss and grief a mother feels as her children become independent and leave home. I am missing them very much, yet I also know that the art of mothering changes continually as one's child grows up. My task is to restrain my desire to detain them, so as to help my sons enter the world without me. The powerful image of the young crocs inside the mother's mouth brings up the terrible mythical potential that parents have – to swallow their children, keeping them from going forth to seek their fortunes. In the Greek myth, the Titan Cronus was told that he would be overthrown by one of his own sons, just as he himself had overthrown his father by castrating him. Psychologically, this is what needs to happen: the young bull takes on the old bull, and there is usually a terrible struggle until the new order is established.

Cronus could not contemplate such a thing. Terrified, wanting to maintain his power, he ate his children one by one as they were born, an image memorably depicted by Goya.

The crocodile taking her young into her mouth is an image of the knife edge between protection and destruction. One moment of going unconscious, and she could swallow and destroy them, incorporating them into her own flesh and image.

The embryo in my back feels safe, however, and she can relax in that fierce embrace. She incubates still, not yet ready to show herself. As I write this, I realise that that is not altogether true. This book itself reveals something of the fearsome tough crocodile and the tender naïve young.

While working with my homeopath friend Dea on symptoms arising from pain in my shoulder joint, I noticed it felt like an injured wing preventing me from flying. I came to a point where I wanted to cry, and experienced a tight, constricting band around my throat. Imagining into the ring which prevented me from swallowing, what came up clearly was a cormorant. I became identified with the banded bird who lives in service to the fisherman, unable to swallow the food she catches.

On returning home, I happened to mention this to a friend who told me that she had recently given away all her videos except for one. It was called *Cormorant Man*, and concerned a Chinese fisherman and his relationship with his birds. On watching it, I was deeply moved. What I had assumed to be an abusive, sterile situation, in this case, was not. There was a patient tending and a symbiosis between a human being and birds that we do not often encounter.

To my delight, one of the ways the Chinese man communicated with the birds while they fished was by dancing on his raft.

***

31. Working with Image

What is the knocking at the door in the night?
Is it somebody wants to do us harm.

No, no, it is the three strange angels.
Admit them, admit them.

D.H. Lawrence[139]

A woman came in for a blood pressure check. She is on treatment for hypertension, but isn't taking her medication correctly. She talked to me about all the difficulties in her life. I asked her whether she was inclined to worry, and she announced with some satisfaction that she was 'the worst worrier in the world'. I commented that that was quite an extreme image to have of herself, and that it most probably wasn't true. There are likely to be many people in the world who worry more than she does. I suggested that she change this image, because it was affecting her health.

The images we have of ourselves and which underlie every aspect of the way we see the world – from money to food – are there whether we notice them or not. We live out of them and in reaction to them continually and largely unconsciously.

I am aware that this is a bold statement. Some people assert that they do not experience this and that they live through feelings, words or thoughts, not images. Yet it is worth examining whether underlying these feelings, words and thoughts are images that arise out of our associations. They are often partial or even distorted. In extreme cases this is blatantly obvious as when an anorexic experiences herself as fat, even as she is dying of starvation. An employer may have an image of himself as a good leader yet comes across as an unfeeling tyrant to his employees, or a pensioner may see himself as worthless, but his grandchildren look forward to visiting him.

***

Marion Milner notes that there is something in her mind that is actively concerned with the truth of experience, yet not through conscious reasoning. This 'something' seems to express itself in terms of images, not arguments.[140]

When we get stuck in our lives or in our art, we might well be using the wrong tool to find what we need. The light of reason can only reveal reasonable answers. Creativity is not sensible.

When we are confronted with a problem or creative task, rather than employing logic to solve the dilemma, we can try to stay with the image it evokes. This demands skills not encouraged in our culture. It requires us to live the question that the image presents without trying to fix, solve, or resolve it, trusting that it will speak to us in its own language, in its own time and on its own terms. We need to be sensate to perceive the image, to tune in with all our senses in order to receive as much information as possible.

One way of looking at a symptom, relationship difficulty or dream is that it is an incomplete glimpse of a particular non-rational force field. As illustrated in the previous chapter, if I had assumed that my sore shoulder was only the result of an inflammatory condition, and that the tightening in my throat was merely a way of restraining my tears, I would not have arrived at the underlying cormorant with its helpful and stress-relieving associations.

Psyche (or soul, the unconscious, or the image), communicates with us through what Mindell calls channels. The six main channels are visual, auditory, movement, proprioceptive (sensations like hot, tight, sharp, full), relationship and world. The first three have inner and outer components; for example, I can see something out in the world, or in my mind's eye.

The cormorant made itself known to me through sensations in both my shoulder and my throat (proprioception). Paying attention to this, the image fleshed itself out into a bird I could see clearly, with an injured wing and a banded throat. Her dark feathers glistened in the sunlight, and she looked about with quick little flicks of her head, blinking her eyes. Water flowed nearby, and she shifted on her perch. The trapped bird in me came alive, and I could feel her more deeply, and feel more deeply for her. Through my friend who gave me the *Cormorant Man* video, where the relationship between bird and man was symbiotic, my associations with entrapment were turned on their head. My fear and sadness were transformed into awe.

Interestingly, the friend who gave me the video has similar entrapment issues. Her mother was incarcerated for years in a concentration camp, and the daughter carries this motif in her flesh. My friendship was another channel through which additional cormorant information was 'downloaded' when the video arrived on cue – what Mindell would describe as the world channel.

Consulting the oracle yields multiple and partial information that arrives in fragments through our different senses, and requires the broad searchlight attention to notice and to value. My relationship with Psyche is like that of the cormorant with the cormorant man, a symbiotic conversation and nourishment. I serve the muse, who feeds me in turn.

When we experience a bodily symptom, or see something or hear a sound that excites or disturbs us, when we make habitual movements, or are embroiled in a relationship difficulty or a problem relating to society, Mindell suggests this is a sensate glimpse of the information that lies behind these clues. A bigger picture can be revealed through employing imagination in all the senses, uncovering the whole image that lies behind a tic, backache or a mugging, to give examples. When we increase the signal by amplifying or inhibiting the disturbance in one sensory channel, the pressure or tension increases until it crosses a threshold. Related material then starts appearing in the other senses. Exploring the same drive through other channels fleshes out the information still further until we stand in the presence of the three-dimensional image of the disturbance. Paying attention to what the image wants, and patiently awaiting answers in its own time and on its own terms, the image starts to shift towards a non-rational resolution.

A gesture can be amplified into dance, and dance into a physical sensation or vision which can be expanded further through painting the dancer or the dance. Sound might arrive as music, or as words or noises vocalised. Writing from the dancer's perspective enlarges the experience, and ushers in more information. Working in this way, we ourselves become more fully human, using creative capacities we have neglected for years.

When we have an initial intimation of an image, there is no way of knowing in advance where the work will lead, as images do not speak through the intellect. Our minds have dominated the way we process our lives for centuries, and for that we have paid a huge price. Intellect is a very valuable instrument, but it is only one out of the entire collection of faculties available to human beings. Initially, while approaching the image, we will ask our analytic minds to be still.

I have likened interpreting the symbol to closing the door prematurely. Another reason not to assign meaning too quickly is that the unconscious can be like a small wild animal that pokes its nose shyly out of its burrow. Approaching a dream or embodied image boldly and arrogantly with the razor of the dissecting mind can cause information from the psyche to hide. The whole animal might be encouraged to reveal itself if we wait quietly and patiently. We need to cultivate humility to be able to sit with the image, not knowing what it means or wants.

We can come to understand ourselves and our motivations better by making the images that underlie everything we do visible, or conscious. We can learn to interact with the richness of symbolic life by stopping to ask: What does the image want?

***

Body as temple, wild animal, soft purse, vessel, stardust, sacrifice, altar, slave, ruin, caryatid, portal, doormat, instrument, drum, survivor, touchstone, lodestone, lighthouse, millstone, poem, cavern, hieroglyph, tomb, effigy, rebel, traitor, conduit, scribe, home.

***

A man led me into a huge cave dimly lit by ambient light. As the darkness settled into shapes, I became aware that it was filled with monkeys. Ahead, seated on a raised ledge, was their leader – a matriarch. She had the clearest eyes I had ever seen, and they were looking directly at me. In my hand, picked up from the ground, were small black oval pellets, and I found that they were olives. I put some into my mouth. They were the most delicious, salty olives I had ever tasted. The floor of the cave was covered with them. As I was savouring one, a bat flitted past. With horror I realised that what I had in my mouth was bat shit.

Or was it?

I did not know, and stood, confused. Were they fabulous olives, or disgusting pellets of bat shit? The queenly monkey, still staring straight at me, was able to differentiate, every time. I woke, understanding my task: to develop the capacity to know the difference between partaking of sacred fruit and eating shit.

The dream images spoke directly to my situation in my midlife crisis. They shook me awake, and assist me to this day.

***

32. In Service

[God] is the name by which I designate all things
that cross my wilful path violently and recklessly,
all things that upset my subjective views, plans
and intentions and change the course of my life
for better or for worse.

Jung[141]

We are all in service to someone or something, whether we
know it or not. It is worth recognising and acknowledging the
nature of one's service. We can create all kinds of difficulties for
ourselves and the planet if we do not.

The ego likes to be in control. Of course, control is a good
thing in many ways: it allows us to apply appropriate restraint,
like not assaulting someone who makes us angry, and not
wetting our undies. But our egos can be little dictators, not
allowing new information in, and manipulating or bullying
others to be in service to our own beliefs and desires.

We are all members of social and political systems that are
in service to something. Government ministers ideally serve the
people, but they could equally be in service to power, money and
their own clique of friends and family. Religious institutions,
constituted to serve deities, their congregations and the tenets
of religious tracts, can be corrupted to serve the ruling dogma.
The hatred, discrimination and vilification that the church has
shown historically towards women, homosexuals and those of
other races and faiths are examples where the church failed in
its service to the spiritual tenets of love.

If society buys into the belief that we are born into a
position in society that God has ordained, it makes the ruling
elite more secure and revolt less likely. Women who accept

everything their husbands decide, or a man who cannot stand up to his abusive boss, are examples of serving patriarchy.

Alcoholics and other substance abusers are in service to their addiction; those people close to them who 'help' them by endlessly forgiving them and lending them money are also in service to the problem.

Compulsive shopping is being in service to our own greed and the worst manipulations of commerce and capitalism, as is corporate refusal to take responsibility for cleaning up pollution and for the abuse of employees. At work, we might be applying ourselves to earning money only, no matter the consequences, or to getting away with as little effort as possible.

Scientists can be in service to ego, capitalism or their own glory. They can enter a curiously amoral, or even immoral territory, where compassion, conscience and restraint can vanish in the quest to be the first to discover something new. The breeding, confinement and torture of animals for experimental purposes, genetic modification, and the use of human embryos for scientific research, throw up the question whether there are occasions where we should restrain from certain actions even though we have the means to initiate them.

What is our guiding light in these matters? The search for scientific truth might sometimes savage another more important truth about how to conduct our lives.

In the poem 'Discovery',[142] Wislawa Szymborska, examines the dilemma. She depicts a man who makes a great discovery, but who secretly destroys his years of work instead of achieving fame and fortune, because he realises that the consequences for the world will be too terrible.

The Dalai Lama has said that we should try to make the world a better place. Many people have dedicated their life's work to discovering or inventing things that some say improve our lives, and others say make things worse. It can be difficult to predict how things are going to turn out so as to avoid serious error, or unintended consequences.

A failure of humankind is to set ourselves above nature, similar to the way the mind is set above the body. We regard the earth as an endless resource we are entitled to. If, instead, we were in service to the earth, our actions would have to change.

***

Jung suggested that the first half of life is an opportunity to explore what we are good at, and to strengthen our egos in the world. He proposed that events in the second half of life call us to turn inward, in order to review who we are and to assess what tasks we have ignored while we established ourselves in work and relationships.[143]

This is not a neat division, and some are called earlier to reconsider their path. His view implies that, at some point, we will all have to reconsider our lives using tools that bear no relation to how we ordinarily measure our progress in the world – via fame, fortune and status. What does life, or Psyche, want of us? Being in service to something other than fame, status and fortune requires acquiescence, willingness and submission. It is likely to lead us through failure and suffering as much as through pleasure and satisfaction.

Being in service to the notion of the muse, or God, or the good of humankind, or of nature, does not in itself mean that we will make the world a better place, as we know from history. The Crusades, the Inquisition, the War on Terror, Nazism, Total Onslaught and Jihad, to name a few, have all been initiatives supposedly in service to the good and/or God.

Yet, What am I in service to? is an important question. It is a question worth living.

***

A writer friend was lamenting his inability to get down to writing commissioned pieces. He noted the irony that this block had occurred only once his writing was recognised and valued. Yet he knew he was born to write. I suggested that a way through the obstructions that unseated his best intentions, was to hold fast to the idea that he was in service to that which needed his participation to get ideas and information onto the page. Being in service would prioritise how he spent his time, effort and money, and allow other hindrances to fall away.

Being in service to something other than one's own ego-desires is a great stress reliever. If I plan a course of action that is important to me, and it doesn't work out, I still feel disappointed. But my distress and frustration is ameliorated by submitting to the thought that perhaps I was rowing up the wrong creek. This opens me to the possibility that something else essential to my course in life may happen, but which I might have been too blinkered by desire and cultural constructs to notice.

If I am in service to something-that-knows-better-than-I-do, this deference must reset the way I approach my life. It effectively deals with the negative critic who continually infers that what I do and how I do it is never good enough, it helps me to pay attention to minimal cues showing me how to proceed, and it requires me to reconsider my priorities.

Being in service requires sacrifice of something held dear by the ego. Stopping habitual activities and making space to render myself available to service initially increases my anxiety – until I find myself in the zone of the download. Then the artist becomes an instrument of the artwork. Success and failure become less important than focusing on the form, content, feeling, tempo and music of the piece arriving onto the page through the conduit of my body.

***

33. The World in a Grain of Sand

I am not the composer of the song of life,
I am but its singer;

Puleng Nkomo[144]

There are tools common to the disciplines of science, art and living creatively: curiosity, observation, a beginner's mind, being prepared to take risks and to be wrong, and imagination.

When Rilke suggested to a young poet that he 'live the questions', he was encouraging an attitude of open-mindedness. He was suggesting that we should not fix our attitudes too quickly, and that, even when we do have strong opinions, we keep a door open for contradiction to enter. He was saying that there are questions that cannot yield simple answers, as they involve complexity and mystery.

Whether we know it or not, many of us have mistaken the questions for answers. We live the hypotheses unquestioningly as though they reflect reality, for example: loyalty is always a good thing, men are violent, children must always be protected, I can't draw, or Chinese people don't care about the environment.

Beliefs, or attitudes, are often extrapolated from a lone experience, or are views adopted from our parents or society. Beliefs are like touchstones. They tell us who we are, what we think and where we belong. They give us identity, inform our decisions and help us feel better because we think we are right. But denial and self-deceit are rife, as is political, economic, religious and relationship manipulation by those who stand to gain if we buy into a particular view of the world. The so-called facts are sometimes right and sometimes wrong, and it is essential to differentiate. If we rephrase attitudes as questions, we can open ourselves to finding out whether they contain any truth.

***

The film maker David Cronenberg commented that we are all mad scientists, experimenting in the lab of life with ways to resolve problems, and to ward off chaos.[145] Yet I am not going to set up a randomised, double-blind controlled trial every time I want to observe whether something is true or not. A simpler method is a reality check, taking stock of both my internal environment and the external situation.

Checking in means pausing to find out how I feel, or how I am managing on the inner front. This is not easy when a complex of emotions is present. But not checking in means that I might go with my usual way of doing things – which might not represent adequately who I am, nor be the best solution to that situation.

A stressed patient of mine who worked as a secretary for a man who was getting divorced was in a hurry to get through her appointment with me as she was worried about being late to pick his children up from school. When I expressed surprise that this was part of her job description, she said she felt sorry for both her boss and for the children. She also realised that her employer was manipulating her capacity for compassion, and had managed to transfer his issues around childcare to her. Checking in, she identified that she habitually tried to save people at her own expense, and was able to access her anger at what was essentially abuse of her position. She resolved to refuse to do personal tasks for him in the future.

When a man complained about suffering from chronic insomnia, I asked him whether there was something that he needed to accomplish in life before he could rest properly. He stopped and thought about it, and then confessed that he needed to finish his doctoral thesis, but had been putting it off. When last I heard, he had completed his thesis and was sleeping well.

I encourage patients who need to lose weight to check in with their bodies to see whether they are hungry before they put food into their mouths. There might be another kind of desire that needs attention. Identifying what that is can be difficult if one has developed bad habits around eating. It is also worth checking in as to whether the food available is even desirable. If you slow down and use your taste buds instead of wolfing the food down, you might discover that the processed food so tantalisingly displayed on television actually tastes like cardboard, or is too sweet.

Checking in is not just about the moment. It is about re-educating our feedback mechanisms. They are innate, but we override them repeatedly. Feedback is the way life prevents one-sidedness and excess. Overstep the mark to the left, and a little helper kicks in to steer us gently to the right. It keeps us on track.

Physiologically, this mechanism is called homeostasis. Chemically, the body cannot survive unless it is kept within narrow margins of temperature, acidity, levels of glucose, biliruben, urea and other by-products of metabolism. From an immunological point of view, symbiotic organisms need to be kept in balance for optimum health and wellbeing. Behaviourally there is a complex interplay of endocrine and neurological guides that ensure that we get off our butts to find food and shelter and mates in order to produce offspring, and also to avoid dangers in the environment.

When we are hungry, a peptide informs us of this, and we eat. When we have had sufficient, another peptide switches off the hunger triggers, and ideally we stop eating. Humans override these natural correctives by eating when we are not hungry: out of boredom, self-hatred, anxiety, obedience, reward, misery, habit, routine, a 'sweet tooth' and politeness.

The stomach – the bag below the diaphragm – expands when we habitually overeat. It then takes even more food to trigger the feeling of fullness, which again we override when our fear of not getting enough, or some equivalent image, causes us to pile the plate with another helping. If we are overweight, training ourselves to eat less will help our natural correctives to re-establish themselves.

A patient of mine describes herself as a chocaholic. Once she starts on a large bar, she cannot stop until it is finished. She has identified this drive as coming from a place of self-hatred. She imagines that when she has eaten her way into diabetes she will feel relief, as she will then have a good reason to hate herself.

Checking in can give us some insight into how we feel and behave, and how that might not be in our best interests. But is insight sufficient for change? My chocaholic patient is still reaching compulsively for the relief of the cocoa bean, still gaining weight, and is still a candidate for developing diabetes. Self-knowledge is insufficient to motivate change where we have not engaged with the underlying image – in this case, one that involves self-hatred. When stressed, she sees herself as a pathetic crying child that must be silenced with food – which was her father's attitude to her. Paying attention to and fleshing out this image could help her to transform both the image and her relationship with chocolate.

Checking out is asking for feedback from sources outside ourselves as to whether our perceptions are accurate. Both checking in and checking out require an attitude of genuine curiosity. They also require ego strength. Most of us don't want feedback. We have been too hurt, too abused. We are defended against hearing how we have made mistakes – also against how wonderful we are. We even have trouble looking in the mirror.

***

Akin to the homeostasis found in our physiology, a kind of homeostasis also operates within the psyche in the form of the daimon, who tries to keep us on track by interrupting us when we wander. He will use anything to capture our attention, throwing things in our path to encourage or discourage: boredom, illness, accidents, disability, invitations in the post, books that fall into our hands, knocks at the door, meeting strangers who speak directly to our passion, unexpected calls to travel, overheard conversations.

We step over many of the gifts offered by the psyche, and they go unnoticed. Staying on track requires developing particular attention to detail so as to pick up minimal cues and to follow them. We become detectives investigating our own lives, the difference being that we are not only trying to track what happened in the past, but trying to track what we might do and be in the future.

This is an aspect of 'living the question', a preoccupation with the subtle, non-verbal conversation that occurs within and without us all the time. The metaphor of a conversation incorporates the idea that we are participants – not dictators, nor passive observers waiting for destiny to descend. Our side of the exchange involves trying out this and that, and then 'listening' for the reply, using all our senses. The reply is the feedback from Psyche, the opening up of fresh vistas, or of repeated blocks, the encouragement to proceed or to change course.

The homeostasis of the psyche is different from the homeostasis of the body. The latter has evolved to keep us within the norm, to keep us normal, our pH at around 7.4, our oxygen saturation at about 98 per cent. The psyche, however, encourages us on the very specific track of what Jung calls individuation[146] – discovering and developing our unique niche in the world.

The guidance of the daimon is very different from the way we have been taught to process information in the rational, sensible world. Following our individual path might look very odd or problematic from the outside. And this is where the tool of checking out requires judicious application. Measuring our perceptions against those of others can be useful, but it can also constrict our lives, maintaining them in service to the cultural, religious and political demands of the time, and dissuading us from being in service to our own unique paths.

As my son said recently, 'I know that this is not a good time financially to make this decision, but it is *my* time'. The confidence with which he said this indicated to me that he was following a directive from his own soul self that knows better than anyone else what he needs, for better or for worse. Psyche, as we have noted, is not interested in outer indicators of success, but in the congruence and confluence of story.

***

Checking in and checking out is a way of becoming aware of excess, and not only in the domain of food.

I was invited to a friend's house to celebrate Pesach one year, something I had never participated in before. I am interested in ritual and ceremony, the ancient glue that binds cultures and religions. I liked the symbolism of the salt and the eggs, I liked the opening of the door to let the spirit of Elijah in, but most of all, I liked the song about enough.

There are two aspects of 'enough' as embodied in the Jewish prayer. One is about an end to slavery, a sense of taking a stand against and escaping from abuse; the other is an acknowledgment of gratitude for having sufficient: I have food on my plate, it is enough; I have a roof over my head, it is enough.

I felt very moved by this, living in a culture where the dominant message is: you do not have enough, you should have more, and more, and you should have it now – more money, more food, a bigger car, a bigger credit limit.

How much is enough? How do we escape from slavery? If we do not heed the early feedback signs of abdominal discomfort or smog, our bodies and the world will speak even louder, through indigestion, rising blood sugar and blood pressure, and increased cancer rates from pollutants. When we consistently ignore these warnings, our bodies give up under the strain, and the protest of 'enough' manifests in disability and death. If we erode the foundation of life on this planet through our wasteful, acquisitive and warring ways, we could destroy the human race, taking other species with us.

The earth will have had enough of us.

***

DAWN GARISCH

34. Living in the Crocodile's Mouth

I load my brain
with all manner of images
this chamber and that

the whole planet is spinning
this is sharper than science

Geoffrey Haresnape[147]

Science confines itself to things that can be measured, yet our lives are shaped both consciously and unconsciously by powerful images. The power of the image or symbol, as anyone knows who has been profoundly affected by a painting, is that it speaks in many tongues. If we do not know something about the motifs that affect us, we will be manipulated and subverted by them. Also, we will have more difficulty in entering a conversation with the force that lives through us, the entity that communicates through images, not words.

Noticing our impulses can put us in touch with this attribute of our psyche. A friend started doing collage after her husband's sudden death. She said later that she chose this medium because she thought it was not real art, but an inferior technique used by children. To her amazement and amusement, she learnt that great artists like Picasso, Matisse and Rego had created renowned and important works using collage. Undervaluing both the medium and her own efforts paradoxically freed her to make the most wonderful art.

Some time afterwards she attended a workshop where the teacher used one of the earliest recorded stories to demonstrate aspects of the feminine. My friend identified with Inanna, who decided to make the difficult descent to the underworld in order to visit her sister, and was rewarded by being dismembered: torn apart into pieces of flesh, which were hung up on meat hooks.

This led her to realise that a central image in her life is the feeling of being torn apart, both in the ongoing experience of physical pain, and in the sense of having difficulty with focus, or centring. Unconsciously she had chosen collage as a means of experiencing both the tearing and dismemberment, as well as the bringing together of the disparate pieces into the container of a new image. Collage, as she has used it, meant taking the old order constructed by others, and disrupting it, rendering it into a chaos of meaningless fragments, out of which she created a new constellation. Here the artist becomes both the destroyer and the creator in equal measure; here the person is no longer a victim of the dynamic of her life; she is engaged in the full spectrum of her experience. She is developing the value of her life motif, working with it rather than against it. Although she is involved in the concrete – tearing and cutting up, and reconstituting images – she is at the same time deeply connected to the symbolic.

Arnold Mindell[148] says that your first childhood dream, as well as your chronic symptoms, are ways of accessing the pattern of your life. In the next chapter, I illustrate my own insights around this interesting idea. Another way is through recalling the fairy tales that spoke powerfully to you as a child. Those stories that charge the imagination and that a child never tires of hearing repeatedly, may stimulate and prefigure the non-rational shape of her life.

The fairy tale that came to me in a workshop on the subject was *Jack and the Beanstalk*. I wished to be the boy my father had always wanted. To my shame, I was terrified of heights. I was the boy sitting at the bottom of the tree, wanting the riches that lay inaccessibly above me. In the story, Jack climbed up and stole them. He was poor, and he risked his life to get riches from the people-eating ogre. A bag of gold, a goose that laid golden eggs, and a harp that played beautiful music. The last one was a surprise to me. If you are starving, I wondered, what is the point of music?

Jack's story for me was one of ambition. As I explored the drama and images, I could feel the fear of rising above my 'station', of poking my head above the clouds, of success. I was writing professionally at that point, wanting to write a great South African novel, at the same time terrified to put myself out there in the world, worried that I was writing drivel, that reviewers would crush me into the ground. Yet Jack innocently, with single-mindedness and the help of the ogre's wife, a good woman in-the-know, went and got what he wanted to help his own sceptical mother. And in the end it was the ogre who fell and died. I wanted to overcome the ogre that tyrannised my inner beanstalk.

I came to understand that the theft of the harp that played exquisite music represented my need to engage in beauty for its own sake, not for riches, security, fame or status. Recognising this has helped me to disengage from the requirements and goals of our society when I need to, and affords me another way to measure how well I am doing.

***

The image of the embryo cradled in the crocodile's mouth arose from my backache while using the tool of embodied imagination. For years I have pondered the nature of the unconscious, whether it is friend or foe, a helpful guide or a destroyer. It can be both. Jung described the psyche, like nature, as amoral. Psyche has no vested interest in good or bad. Yet, as in the body, there does seem to be a trend towards healing, or completeness. Our bodies mostly want to get better, and work hard to do this, despite the ways we live that are contrary to this drive. Psyche also presents opportunities for us to heal from past traumas and to seize our lives, but we often use our imaginations to give us reason to avoid seeking help.

A crocodile is one of the fiercest and most formidable creatures on earth. It has survived and flourished in the same form for millennia. When I look at a crocodile, I read: Don't mess with me. At the same time, the crocodile can hold its young protectively in its mouth without killing them, carrying them from their hatching place on the bank to the safety of the river. I love this image. In contrast, those images espoused by most spiritual paradigms are of goodness and light. They don't speak to me. I need a guide that can turn ugly if necessary, that arises out of the wisdom of mud.

I have often been described as fierce[4] during my life. It is not something I have recognised in myself. Lately, though, I have come to appreciate this. I am becoming less shy to give off the vibe, Don't mess with me, and increasingly able to adopt an attitude of polite ice towards people whom I cannot trust or who have repeatedly wronged me. I am able to get tough, particularly when my young are threatened. My sons are grown now, and can largely look after themselves. The ongoing young in my care are new beginnings and inspirations – the sense of a flickering flame I protect with cupped hands.

***

A journalist friend of mine was constructing a website, partly to promote her work, which includes two books of non-fiction, and partly to gather together in one place the many things that she has written during her life. She emailed me, conflicted about how to define herself in this public space. 'Should I describe myself as a poet?' she worried. At that point she had not yet had any of her poetry published. Although she acknowledged that reading and writing poetry is central to her life, she felt it was arrogant, even fraudulent, to call herself a poet.

---

[4] I realised the other day that the words fire and ice contain all the letters that comprise 'fierce'.

Many of us are stopped in our tracks by the feeling that we dare not call ourselves artists. We are almost embarrassed to admit that we play guitar, or paint, or write. We have a notion that the 'the real thing' is 'out there', and we are reluctant to expose our efforts, fearing they would fail dismally if judged against the greatest artists, writers and composers of all time.

This attitude is truly damaging to creativity in all of us. More importantly, it is insulting to the muse, who needs the attentive collaboration of humans to channel her expression into the physical world.

I told my friend that the way to evaluate whether she was a poet or not was to answer the question: Do you see life as a poet? What I meant by that was: do invigorating phrases present themselves insistently to you? Are you sensitive to the underbelly inherent in situations? Do juxtapositions of objects or events 'speak' to you in such a way that you want to record them? Do you derive huge satisfaction – no, more than that, do you experience relief – from finding an exact combination of words that manage to evoke something that can barely be described? Are you frequently attempting to distil emotions and experience into a verbal elixir that directs you and others towards something valuable and true, spiralling towards the ineluctable centre, yet not pinning it down and rendering it lifeless? Are you reading the radical subtext embedded in the everyday? Are you busy with what Kafka calls the axe for the frozen sea within? Are you driven to solve the commotion within your chest by taking up a pen? Do you live life in the world while being rooted in the symbolic? Karin immediately understood what I meant, and went ahead to describe herself as a poet on her webpage.

Seeing life as an artist means cultivating a certain kind of attention. Anyone can develop this way of being and seeing. We all have patterns to our lives, whether we notice them or not. To some, this noticing comes naturally. There are those who can track their creative passage back to their first memories and dreams.

An example is the ceramicist Christina Bryer who grew up on a farm, and who loved to play in the mud and sand at the dam. One of her earliest pre-school recollections was of the linoleum on the floor of her bedroom. It was turquoise blue, and decorated with nursery rhymes. She recalls illustrations of men in a tub, and a girl being frightened by a spider, and a boy sitting in a corner, but these images did not impress her. When her mother read the rhymes out to her, she was even more puzzled. Why would three men want to be in a tub? What did 'intsy wintsy' mean? What on earth was a tuffet, and why would the boy want to sit in a corner?

The rhymes made no sense to her, but what did intrigue her was the border pattern of a double helix – a rope twined again around itself – and decorative stars. There were five-pointed and six-pointed stars, and she soon worked out that when she traced the five-pointed stars with her finger, the pattern went on indefinitely, whereas, with the six-pointed stars, after three points you had to lift your finger or pencil to draw the other three points which went off in the opposite directions. When she asked adults whether they wanted her to draw a five- or six-pointed star, they said it didn't matter, which she knew was astonishing nonsense – it made all the difference in the world! When she first came across the sign for infinity, it made complete sense to her; it was the same principle as the five-pointed star, where, once your finger started travelling, it could carry on forever.

These early preoccupations have converged in later life into an artistic style where she incorporates geometric aperiodic patterns into the ceramic plates she makes. Aperiodic means that the pattern lacks any translational symmetry – a shifted copy will never match the original. Christina explains that geometry is a spiritual practice. 'The discipline of the form gets the ego out of the way,' she says. 'I am not one of those expressive artists who wakes up in the morning wondering what I am going to do today. Starting with the absolute of the grid frees you to work with infinite possibilities. If I'd had a different daimon, I would have noticed the pictures, or the writing on the linoleum, but it was the pattern that fascinated me. I work with the same principles of harmony and beauty that can be found in peasant music and craft all over the world.'

***

35. Recapturing the Original Plan

Each day the lawn spits up bits of broken glass
Colleen Higgs[149]

The daimon, or a calling, or the idea that we are living symbolic, teleological lives implies a thread or plot that starts way back in childhood.

I am going to compare living life to engaging with a story. E. M. Forster, in his book *Aspects of the Novel*, says that there are two ways of reading a book. One way only requires enough tension in the story to keep you curious, reading to find out what is going to happen next, right on until the end, whereupon you close the lid of the book and bury it back into the bookshelf.

The other way of approaching story requires the reader to maintain two selves, one that is immersed in the text and what happens next, and the other to keep track of developments from a slight remove. This latter self is able to hold in his mind an overview of all the happenings, from which he can start to make connections and see patterns emerging. Whether or not a novel has a bigger picture with subtext is one of the elements that distinguish literature from pulp fiction.

It is possible to live our lives engaged only with a superficial reading of our own text, without paying attention to the overarching plot, the sub-plots, undercurrents, and the patterns emerging. Living the surface story, with the trundle of 'and then, and then, and then' means that we become expert floaters, estranged from our own beautiful and terrible depths. Staying with veneer means we might live with sterile, one-sided images – images that have been appropriated by the rational. This pinning down of the symbol by affixing to it only one tangible fact occurs in religion, where Christian fundamentalists use the story of Adam and Eve to deny all the evidence for the theory of evolution, and thereby give evolutionists ammunition for dismissing all theology.

Christ on the cross, the Buddha under the tree, the lotus flower, the holy black stone of Islam and the virgin birth are all examples of symbols that contain mysterious meanings and resonance. They have survived for centuries precisely because they speak powerfully to aspects of our lives.

***

A life is a story, and biography and autobiography are amongst the most popular genres. A good life, we must remind ourselves, is usually not a bland or uneventful one. Just as one needs all the instruments and all the notes, high and low, to create a beautiful and memorable symphony, the composition of a life will necessitate both joy and grief.

I could not have written this book without the chequered past I have had – training in fields as diverse as statistical methods in occupational research, movement therapy, and script writing, and employment in situations as different as emergency units, memoir workshops and academia. My illness and my son's fall have also shaped my life. All the seemingly disparate aspects of my life that appear random have built towards and been threaded together by this project. Some would argue that I have merely found a way to put the accidental bits of my life together, but the sense I have from inside my life is that of guidance, of serving some impulse that requires expression. It feels as though this book and the subjects it tackles lie squarely on the path of what I was born for, even though it was not until very recently that I even considered writing non-fiction.

Perhaps that is a reason why midlife is time for pause and reflection; by then one has lived long enough to note patterns, and to have gathered together a range of experience and skill which, on careful reassessment, might bear the markings of the daimon. They could be signposts helping us to notice where we are going.

***

Second time round and one year later, I am grateful to receive news that I have been awarded two grants to complete this book. It means that I can buy the time to do further research and editing so as to do this project justice. It means that others have deemed this work of non-fiction worthy of their money. It provides assistance to pursue further what I was born to do.

As soon as I write this, I feel the cringe of the fear of inflation. Who am I to say what I was born for? Yet while I am applying myself to the task of writing down and sorting out on the page these things I am fired up about, I feel alive and engaged. I feel supported and accompanied. This does not even feel like work, although I am working hard.

The grant is positive feedback from the world. Checking in, I feel fortunate, determined. Checking out, I have more books to read, more ideas to wrestle with, and a couple of interviews to set up.

***

36. Changing the End of the Story

The only thing to do is to keep still, to hold still at any price
To learn to contain ourselves.
So that in the long pause the instincts can
    reassert themselves
And our intuition can come to life and give us direction.
For at the present in the whirring insanity of mental
    consciousness
We violate ourselves every moment, and violate
    everybody else
In a cog-wheel clatter of violation.

D. H. Lawrence[173]

Augusten Burroughs, who writes memoir, recounts the moment he realised that he should write. He was on his second litre of alcohol, trying to obliterate the anxiety that dominated his life since his unstable and abusive childhood. He describes not being able to get to the 'safe place' through drinking that night. In desperation, he switched on the television. There was a programme on about Eisenhower, who was quoted as saying: 'Every gun that is made, every battleship that is built, every missile that is launched, is a direct theft from the people who are hungry and starving in this world.'

These words moved Burroughs to get up and go to the computer and start to write. He suddenly saw that there were truths and a complexity to life that he was not engaging with; instead he was drinking himself into a stupor and distracting himself with the Internet.

He describes in some detail how he turned his life around by putting his thoughts and worries down on the page. The charge he got from writing made him feel alive, and helped him give up the lifestyle that was not only killing him, but shutting him down.[150]

***

In *Why Good People Do Bad Things*,[151] Hollis shows how we are owned by the anxiety management plan we evolved to survive the vicissitudes of childhood. The strategies we put in place may have kept our heads above water back then, but as adults they might well drown us. Our behaviours and attitudes have become ingrained over years and years of habit. When attempting to alter the way we do things, it is too easy to fall back into the deep grooves of our old ways.

Neuroscientists have shown that the brain retains the ability to change throughout a lifetime.[152] We are able to develop healthy neural pathways in adulthood even if these were not established when we were babies. This remodelling of the dysfunctional brain takes place within an empathetic relationship. Schore[153] shows that much of the healing in psychotherapy occurs subliminally between therapist's and client's right hemispheres. He calls this subliminal empathy 'unconscious imagination'. The integrity of the therapist's right hemisphere – in other words, her capacity for relationship – to a large extent determines whether the results of adverse early experience in the patient's brain can be undone.

This healing of destructive thought patterns also happens outside of therapy. What it requires is that someone cares enough about my wellbeing to both empathise with my pain, and challenge me about my bad habits, for long enough for new patterns of thinking to develop. The simple yet difficult task of the constant gardener.

The psychiatrist, Louis Cozolino,[154] has shown that an individual's capacity for change is dependent on his ability 1) to tolerate anxiety, 2) without knowing what is going to happen next, and 3) for long enough for new neural pathways to connect in the brain. Altering your habitual way of thinking and doing things comes down to *literally* changing your mind: constructing new synapses and even new neurons within the brain. This is what allows a different pathway to supersede the old way of thinking, feeling and acting. If we cannot tolerate the anxiety of the unknown, we will automatically fall back into old patterns.

These are profound discoveries, and encouraging ones. It means that in order to improve our lives, we first need to understand that we are anxious beings, whether we are aware of this or not. Secondly, we need to recognise that very early on we put unconscious strategies in place to manage this anxiety, and that they are causing us and our relationships grief. Thirdly, if we are going to change our problematic ways – in other words, give up our habitual anxiety management plan – this in itself will unleash a huge amount of anxiety as we hang in the void of what we have been trying to avoid. Finally – and this is the good news – if we can find non-destructive ways to help us through this maelstrom we will emerge on the other side with altered neural patterns, together with the changed behaviour that goes with it.

Augusten Burroughs' anxiety management plan was an extreme one. As an alcoholic, he was slowly killing himself. Yet, on that day he was receptive to change. He observed that he needed to write, even if all that the writing did was to help him deal with the fear he knew was gnawing just below his drunken stupor. He is now an internationally acclaimed author.

***

Plans themselves can be anxiety management strategies. We set a goal and go for that ending. Yet plans often don't work out. Repeatedly failing to get into a branch of study, or recurrent illness, or a relationship that keeps unravelling despite our best efforts, is usually experienced as misfortune. But what if these are the methods the daimon uses to encourage us onto a road we would never have chosen for ourselves, but which leads to a different fortune? Our egos tend not to notice as we are too busy making plans. Plans can arise out of unconscious motivations like boredom or fear which have nothing to do with waking up to our lives and what our lives want of us.

I am all for trying as hard as I can to get something that I really desire, but if I fail to achieve it, it is worth considering that I might be on the wrong track. Negative feedback from life pushes me away, saying no through means other than language. Positive feedback pulls me in, towards itself. It says a big symbolic yes.

Plans are a good starting place for the artist, but rigid plans can result in writing a book or living a life that never realises its full potential. We need both stability and adventure, routine and surprises, choice and destiny. While going all out in the direction of our goals, some part of us can be keeping the eye of the broad searchlight open for what else is going on in the inner and outer landscapes.

The theory of feedback from the psyche is not verifiable, but it is not a bad way to live, and we all have to live by something. Instead of spending the rest of my life resentful and thwarted, still focused on whatever it was that I could not get, I might accept the turn of events that blocks my planned path. I might start paying attention to picking up on the alternative track that opens up.

However, feedback in an abusive situation might come from a person who is manipulating you. The distinction of when to heed feedback and when not to can be clarified by answering the question 'what are you in service to?' Great literature has been written under pain of death or imprisonment. Mandela, Gandhi and Frankl have lived inspiring lives by not succumbing in situations of terrible hardship and injustice, precisely because they did not obey the repetitive and focused negative feedback of abuse, but instead followed the positive feedback and encouragement of a force that lives through them.

Anxiety is a potent activator. It propels us towards the action we know has always given us immediate, short-term, relief. Our original anxieties will naturally arise once we withdraw our habitual management plans: excesses of eating, shouting at the kids, smoking, drugs, visiting the doctor, working long hours, the Internet, porn, drinking, cleaning, shopping, computer games, staying in bed, reading, sex and sport, amongst others. The hiatus we create when we refrain from destructive habits will require curiosity and courage.

In C. S. Lewis's novel on envy disguised as love, *Till We Have Faces*, Orual comes to understand the destruction she has brought about when she writes the history of her time. She notes that writing changed her perception about what had happened, as though the gods were using her pen to operate on her.[155]

Paying attention to the force that lives through us, and following the creative impulse onto the page, stage, into voice or clay is a powerful non-medicinal stress-reliever. The creative act provides an alternative focus, and safe container to turn to while the instincts reassert themselves, and new brain circuits develop. It gives us a medium, a method and tools for working with unpleasant feelings and the unknown, and provides comfort while we wait for our brains and instincts to make the links, connecting us to the authentic. It sets us on a valuable track into our own uncharted territory.

***

37. Of Knives and Glue

When we try to pick out anything by itself, we find
it is tied to everything else in the universe.

John Muir[156]

Astonishing things are happening on the genetic front. The end
is being converted back into the beginning.

A future person consists of one fertilized cell which then
repeatedly divides into a clump of cells termed a zygote. At an
eight cell stage, all the cells are the same. They are all what is
called pluripotential, in that they have the potential to become
anything – a heart cell, a bone cell, a skin cell or a neuron. At
this point, if the zygote is grown in a Petri dish in a laboratory,
it is possible for a scientist to extract one of the cells and send it
off for genetic testing without affecting the organism. One out
of the eight cells can be removed, and the future person will not
be born without an arm or a liver or an eye.

After sixteen weeks of pregnancy, the entire human being
is fully formed. The original pluripotential cells have divided
a zillion times and all have been fixed as to their system and
function. They have had most of their potential permanently
switched off. Although all the chromosomes in each cell contain
the same sequence of genetic information, only some genes are
allowed expression. So, although a bladder wall cell has the
DNA potential to produce bile, it does not, as all the genetic
codes other than that for bladder wall function have been
switched off. End of story.

Or not.

Recently scientists have found ways of switching genetic
material back on, so as to reverse this specialisation. They

can induce a dead-end bladder cell nucleus to return to a pluripotential cell, and engineer it to behave as though it is a freshly fertilised ovum. This is how Dolly the sheep was cloned.

These developments are aspects of an exploding new technology of stem cell research and genetic engineering. It is receiving massive funding at present, and is seen as the major way forward in both health and industry. For example, endocrine cells in the pancreas are part of the endocrine system, and produce a hormone called insulin which is released into the bloodstream to control levels of glucose. Other cells in the pancreas, exocrine cells, are part of the digestive system, and they produce an enzyme called amylase, released into the small intestine to assist the digestion of fats.

Diabetes is the failure of endocrine cells to produce sufficient insulin. Millions of people must take medicine or inject themselves every day to correct this.

The neuroscientist, Qiao Zhou, has found a way to convert exocrine cells into endocrine cells in vitro in the laboratory. This could be a major break-through for diabetes treatment.[157]

Researchers have now found the gene responsible for the spider web protein, and inserted it into goats' embryos. The resultant goats produce milk containing spider web protein – the strongest and most elastic substance for its weight that exists on earth. The protein can be used for sutures and joint replacements, as well as in aircraft and bullet-proof vests.[158]

***

IGem is an international competition for post-grad students held annually at MIT university. The team of students who genetically engineer a unicellular organism with the most innovative outcome is the winner.

Note: if you cannot speak a human language, you will not be able to give informed consent to a procedure or experiment.

You are therefore not consulted before humans alter you or your offspring irrevocably.

A researcher I read about decided to genetically engineer a hairless, glow-in-the-dark rabbit for the amusement of his kids. He clearly does not think there is a problem with that; one could argue that we are just pushing genes around. One could also propose, as some scientists do, that it is better to use surplus human embryos created from artificial fertilization in treating infertility, for experimentation, rather than the current practice of discarding them. Nature, after all, is wasteful of gametes, and miscarriages are common. An eight cell zygote in a Petri dish does not constitute viable life, and many would argue that it cannot be regarded as human. So why throw zygotes in the bin, rather than using them to improve the lives of those who are living?

The rational is not always ethical. Progress could also be a big step backwards. Even breakthroughs like genetically modifying goats to become spider web protein factories should give us reason to pause. As when we discovered how to split the atom, progress in the modern age contains its shadow. We are irrevocably altering the genetic base out of which we live. Our brilliance might well come back to bite us.

***

Our civilization, with its outstanding achievements, has got to this point at a crippling cost. It is difficult to celebrate while the house is on fire.

For too long we have patted ourselves on the back without looking up from the banquet table. We have measured the resources of the world, stripped the earth bare and put it and all that live on her to work for us. We have assumed that all life should be in service to our needs, our health and our wealth, from rats in laboratories, to lions on hunting farms, to the pigs who are farmed underground. We count the profit, but avoid the true costs. We know the price of things we manufacture, but do not consider the value of that we destroy.

Attendant on the recent financial crash, it is abundantly clear that we need alternative measures of health and growth. If the way our communities run is sick, how can we be healthy?

***

Nature, if given a chance, restores itself. Mostly, the body has a drive to get better. The psyche wants to heal. They would fare better if we helped our fragile tissues, and if we plucked up the courage to follow the tracks of our own bloody wounds all the way back to the initial childhood injury.

Our lives would be different if we worked together with earth systems and with our own flesh and blood, rather than against them. If we took care of our planet, nurtured ourselves, and befriended our bodies, our only steadfast companion throughout the whole of our lives, we could turn the relationship into one of partners, or allies.

Science is a valuable tool for approaching these problems. Logos, or logic, is the cutter, objectively dissecting out information and being incisive. Yet we also need Eros, or libido – the glue[159] of relatedness and of the symbolic – to make good choices.

***

Science and technology have only recently come to dominate; previously, in Western history, the arts reigned supreme. Theology and the Greek and Roman Classics were the subjects deemed worthy of study at university. When scientific method first poked its head out of the primordial soup, it was looked on askance. It was not considered a worthy subject for the sons and daughters of the elite to sign on for.

Science has subsequently taken its revenge. Now the Humanities and the Arts are the poor cousins, hanging on to the coat-tails of those disciplines that experiment and measure by reformulating themselves. Social sciences, psychology as science, the human sciences have adopted the name and methodology in an attempt to be taken seriously.

Yet, as any scholar of literature knows, there are other kinds of evidence. A text can provide the mesh through which we glimpse something about ourselves that we recognise. A friend in academia pointed out that literary criticism and translation train the mind in evaluating evidence. As one can misdiagnose a condition by misreading the symptoms, signs, and even the results, one can also misread a text.

***

We are starting to appreciate better the symbolic aspect of life, and find ways of working with it – conversing with the rich, diverse and shifting populace of images. We will come to recognise, once again, as our cave-dwelling ancestors axiomatically did, that the dream/stories that thread our nights, our symptoms, our relationships, our conflicts, our songs and our dances are the stuff our lives are made on.

***

38. Endings

And this above all: to thine own self be true,
and it shall follow, as the day the night,
thou can'st not then be false to any man.

Shakespeare[160]

My mother died a few months ago. At ninety-three, she got the ending she wanted: a sudden death in her own home. I have a strange sense of being severed, or uprooted – my fine root hairs naked and vulnerable on the air. The story of her life has ended; the lid of the coffin has closed on her like the back cover of a book. Her body is turned to ash, scattered back into the landscape. I can never again return to that home.

My mother's voice was the main critic in my head while I wrote. I would worry whenever something sexual turned up on the page. I would warn her: 'I suggest you don't read this, Ma. You are not going to like it.'

'Why ever not?' she would object.

'Because one of the things it deals with is sexuality, Ma. You know you don't like books about that.'

She would harrumph, and look anxious.

I would try to explain: 'We cannot leave subjects as important as sex to the pornographers and the advertisers. Look, and you'll see. Sex is everywhere, trivialised and commodified. Serious writers have to take this on.'

She always read what I wrote, and she coped much better with her errant daughter's outpourings than I gave her credit for. Except for one piece. I decided she would never find out about the short story in an anthology of women's erotica.

Writing with my mother in mind, with trepidation, was my growing edge. It was my opportunity to get real with her. This is who your daughter is, my books announced. This is what preoccupies her, and how she thinks. This is her experiment. It was also my opportunity to get real with myself, and to find out what I am capable of. If I had let the inner mother's voice stop me, I would not have done my life's work.

She was looking forward to reading this book.

Now she's gone.

My body/ my home/ strange planet I inhabit/ old friend/ tough teacher/ worn blanket of flesh. Please can you tell me / how much story I have left?

I want to live a good tale. I want to live deeply, keeping track of the unfolding plot of my life. I want to keep a conversation going with the force that lives through me, to be true to my own story. It is the well from which I drink. Looking back, I see how my life has been threaded through with several motifs, themes that have shaped both me and my writing.

My early dream of fire and ice set one of my patterns going. It has evolved into a fierce presence; also into a small flame kept alive between cupped hands in the frozen wastes of boarding school. My autoimmune disease creates a burning pain in my back and inflammation in my eyes; the damage in my eyes creates an image of a burning bush that is never consumed. Becoming a creative and sexual woman ignited the fire of desire which conflicted uncomfortably with the ice of being a nice girl. My unexpected trip to Antarctica plotted an external journey into ice, into which I carried the small flame of my healing.

I look back with compassion on the woman who has taken these and other themes and images, and penned them to paper, trying to divine who she is and track where she is going. A woman who has found a home in Psyche, which provides nourishment and holding in times of plenty, and offers a reliable lifeline when life feels overwhelming.

Psyche, working through me, reveals me to myself. She connects me to my life plots through image-making – dance, drawing and writing – thus showing me the way back to myself, and stimulating my brain to heal my thinking.

This book is nearly finished. Once I have let the kind and strict critics in, once I have done rewrites and edits, once it is sent off to agents and publishers and I have spent a period gardening, listening to music, resting and feeling mildly depressed – which I remind myself is natural at the end of a big work – what then?

I have a folder full of ideas, but none of them is speaking to me, none holds the essential energy. It is too early. One thing I know is that life will show me. The phone will ring, or I'll have a dream, or I'll overhear a conversation, and I'll be off, my fingers working the Braille trail, trying to decipher what life and books want of me.

Living the question. Creating the days and pages of my life as a conversation with a force that lives through me, until the very last full stop at the end of my final chapter.

THE END

Endnotes

1. Geoffrey Godbert, 'Even on such a Memorable Day,' in Carapace 73:8. Courtesy the poet.
2. W. H. Murray, 1951, The Scottish Himalayan Expedition (London: Dent).
3. Piet Hein, Danish mathematician, physicist, philosopher, writer and creator of puzzles and games. Courtesy Piet Hein's son.
4. Turner et al, 2008, 'Selective Publication of Antidepressant Trails and Its Influence on Apparent Efficacy', New England Journal, Vol. 358:252–260
5. Jerome Groopman, 2006, The Anatomy of Hope (Pocket Books).
6. Phillippa Yaa de Villiers, 2010, from 'The Quiet Conversation', The Everyday Wife (Modjaji Books): 76. Courtesy the poet.
7. Carl Sagan, 'The Burden of Skepticism', The Skeptical Inquirer, Fall 87.
8. W. B. Yeats, 1996, excerpt from 'A Prayer for Old Age', The Collected Poems of W. B. Yeats (Scribner): 282.
9. Carl Gustav Jung, C. G. Zarathrustra Seminar, Princeton University.
10. John Mack, 'In the Mind's Eye', The Museum of the Mind: Art and Memory in World Cultures (London: British Museum Press): 25.
11. Jean-Pierre Changeux, 2005, The Neurobiology of Human Values (Berlin: Springer-Verlag): 1.
12. Mark Solms, 2002, The Brain and the Inner World (New York: Other Press): 5.
13. Louis Cozolino, 2002, The Neuroscience of Psychotherapy (New York: W. W. Norton & company).
14. Candace Pert, 1997, Molecules of Emotion (New York: Scribner).

15. Jean-Pierre Changeux, 2004, The Physiology of Truth (Harvard University Press).

16. James Hillman, 1997, The Soul's Code (Warner Books).

17. Eugene Gendlin, 1982, Focusing (Bantam Books).

18. Helen Luke, 2000, Such Stuff as Dreams are Made On (Parabola Books).

19. Marion Milner, 1986, An Experiment in Leisure (Virago Press Ltd.): ix.

20. Werner Herzog (wikiquote).

21. Dawn Garisch, 2011, Difficult Gifts (Cape Town: Modjaji Books): 8.

22. Ivan Vladislavic, 2006, Portrait With Keys (Umuzi): 108. Courtesy the author.

23. Carl Gustav Jung, 1981, Collected Works, Vol. 13:37 (Routledge & Kegan Paul).

24. A. J. Twerski, 1997, Addictive Thinking: Understanding Self-Deception (Hazeldon): 102–3.

25. James Joyce, 1926, referring to Finnegans Wake in a letter to Harriet Shaw Weaver.

26. William Shakespeare, As You Like It, Act II, sc vii.

27. Ken Barris, 1993, Advertisement for Air (Snailpress): 8. Courtesy the poet.

28. Arnold Mindell, 1986, Working With The Dreaming Body (Routledge & Kegan Paul): 7–9.

29. Siddiq Khan, from 'Blues for the Maid of New Orleans', New Contrast 155:14. Courtesy the poet.

30. May Swenson, 1994, 'Question', Nature: Poems Old and New (Houghton Mifflin): 45. Reprinted with permission of The Literary Estate of May Swenson. All rights reserved.

31. James Joyce, 1991, Dubliners (Signet Classic): 108.

32. Lewis Hyde, 1999, The Trickster Makes This World (North Point Press). 27.

33. M. Scott Peck, 2003, The Road Less Travelled (Touchstone): 15.

34. Michael Cope, YouTube (http://www.youtube.com/watch?v=zO10bs-JHUU). Courtesy the poet.

35. James Hollis, 2007, Why Good People Do Bad Things (Gotham Books/Penguin): 67–68.

36. J. Z. Young, 1987, Philosophy and the Brain (New York: Oxford University Press): 28.

37. Jonas Salk, quoted in Ken Robinson, 2009, The Element (Allen Lane, Penguin Books): 259.

38. Julian David, 2003, 'The Problem of the Feminine in a Patriarchal Culture,' Mantis 15:20–21.

39. Ingrid De Kock, 2002, from 'Inner Note,' Transfer (Cape Town: Snailpress): 50. Courtesy the publisher.

40. Seitlhamo Motsapi, 2002, from 'River Robert,' It All Begins: Poems from Post-liberation South Africa, edited by R. Berold (Gecko Press): 209. Courtesy the publisher.

41. Jean-Pierre Changeux, 2004, The Physiology of Truth: Neuroscience and Human Knowledge (Harvard University Press).

42. Joan Metelerkamp, 2000, from 'Song of marriage', Into the day breaking, Gecko Poetry: 101-2. Courtesy the poet.

43. Antonio Damasio, 1999, The Feeling Of What Happens: The Body And Emotions In The Making Of Consciousness (Harcourt, Bruce and Company): 41.

44. Antonio Damasio, 1999, The Feeling Of What Happens: The Body And Emotions In The Making Of Consciousness (Harcourt, Bruce and Company): 31.

45. M. Solms and O. Turnbull, 2002, The Brain and the Inner World (New York: Other Press).

46. M. Teicher, 'Wounds that time won't heal: the neurobiology of child abuse,' in Cerebrum (2) 4:50–67.

47. Megan Gunnar, quoted in 'The Bond Between Mother and Child,' by Beth Azar, (http://mothersoflostchildren.wordpress.com/2009/03/18/the-bond-between-mother-and-child/).

48. Damasio, The Feeling: 24.

49. Alan Finlay, 2010, Pushing from the Riverbank (Dye Hard Press): 41–42. Courtesy the poet.

50. J. M. Burns and R. H. Swerdlow, 2003, 'Right Orbitofrontal Tumor With Pedophilia Symptom and Constructional Apraxia Sign,' in Archives of Neurology, 60:437–40.

51. Candace Pert, 1997, Molecules of Emotion (New York: Scribner): 139.

52. Pert, Molecules: 270.

53. Kai Lossgott, from 'gentlemenagerie', http://www.kailossgott.com/poetry.html. Courtesy the poet.

54. Hollis, Bad Things: 199–200.

55. Garisch, Difficult Gifts: 24.

56. Antonio Machado, from 'Fourteen poems chosen from "Moral Proverbs and Folk Songs"', Times alone: Selected poems of Antonio Machado © Antonio Machado, translation © 1983 by Robert Bly. Reprinted by permission of Wesleyan University Press (www.wesleyan.edu/wespress).

57. Extracts published in The Sunday Independent, 17 July 2005.

58. James Hillman, 1964, The Guild of Pastoral Psychology: Lecture No. 128: 66–8.

59. Harold Pinter, http://nobelprize.org/nobel_prizes/literature/laureates/2005/pinter-lecture-e.html

60. Noam Chomsky, 2005, Doctrines and Visions (Pocket Penguin 42): 11.

61. James Hillman, 1988, 'And Huge is Ugly,' Tenth Annual E. F. Schumacher Memorial lecture, Bristol, England.

62. Hillman, And Huge.

63. John Lukacs, 1994, Historical Consciousness (New Brunswick, N. J.: Transaction): 358.

64. George W. Lowis,1993, 'Epidemiology of puerperal fever,' Medical History, 37:399–410.

65. Milner, An Experiment: 133–4.

66. Enrico Fermi, http://en.wikiquote.org/wiki/Enrico_Fermi

67. Qur'an 17:36.

68. Bradley Steffens, 'Who Was the First Scientist?' Ezine Article (www.ezinearticles.com).

69. Steffens, 'First Scientist.'

70. H. K. Beecher, 1955, 'The Powerful Placebo,' in JAMA Vol. 159, No. 17.

71. D. H. Newman, 2008, Hippocrates' Shadow (Scribner): 134–59.

72. Hermann Joseph Muller (1890–1967), United States geneticist, who won the Novel Prize for Medicine in 1946.

73. Dr Marcia Angell, 2009, 'Drug Companies & Doctors: A Story of Corruption,' in The New York Review of Books, Jan 15 – Feb 11: 8.

74. Angell, 'Drug Companies': 12.

75. Angell, 'Drug Companies': 12.

76. Mxolisi Nyezwa, 2008, New Country (University of Kwazulu-Natal Press): 40. Courtesy the poet.

77. R. B. Bausell, 2007, Snake Oil Science (USA: Oxford University Press).

78. Turner et al, 'Selective Publication,' 358:252–60.

79. http://clinicalevidence.bmj.com/downloads/25-03-09.pdf.

80. 'Royal College of Physicians: Sir Michael Rawlins attacks traditional ways of assessing evidence,' 16 October 2008, www.politics.co.uk.

81. Jeffrey Bland, 2008, 'Does Complementary and Alternative Medicine Represent Only Placebo Therapies,' Alternative Therapies in Health and Medicine 14(2):16–18.

82. Milner, An Experiment: 34.

83. Carl Gustav Jung, Psychology and Alchemy: 32.

84. Joseph Campbell, 1968, The Hero With A Thousand Faces (Pantheon Books): 91.

85. Mindell, Dreaming Body: 67.

86. Lyn Cowan, 2002, Tracking the White Rabbit: A Subversive View Of Modern Culture (Routledge): 20.

87. Hyde, Trickster: 123.

88. Christine M. Coates, 2011, from 'Remembering Afghanistan, The Sol Plaatje EU Poetry Anthology (Jacana Media): 4. Courtesy the poet.

89. Cowan, White Rabbit: 14.

90. Anthony Storr, 'The Significance of Music,' in Music and the Mind: 177.

91. Aaron Copland, 1952, 'Music and Imagination,' Newton Lectures.

92. Barbara Kingsolver, 2002, Small Wonder (Faber & Faber): 229.

93. Joan Metelerkamp, 2009, from 'Points on poems', Burnt Offering (Cape Town: Modjaji Books): 17–18. Courtesy the poet.

94. Doris Lessing, 1996, Putting the Questions Differently (Flamingo (HarperCollins).

95. E. L. Doctorow, http://thinkexist.com/quotes/e._l._doctorow/.

96. Harold Pinter, http://nobelprize.org/nobel_prizes/literature/laureates/2005/pinter-lecture-e.html.

97. John Fowles, 1997, Wormholes: Essays and Occasional Writings (Jonathan Cape Ltd.).

98. Al Alvarez, 2006, The Writer's Voice (Bloomsbury Publishing): 29.

99. Alvarez, Writer's Voice: 23.

100. Sondra Perl, 'The Composing Process of Unskilled College Writers,' Research in the Teaching of English 13:317–36.

101. Milner, An Experiment: 52.

102. Rainer Maria Rilke, 1986, Letters To A Young Poet (Vintage Books): 34-35.

103. Theodore Roethke, 1974, The Collected Poems of Theodore Roethke (Random House): 49.

104. http://www.sheilachandra.com/albums/bonecrone.php.

105. http://www.guardian.co.uk/books/2007/dec/08/nobelprize.classics.

106. Rilke, Letters: 23–25.

107. Gus Ferguson, 'Endgame', Carapace 73. Courtesy the poet.

108. Paul Ashton, 2007, From the Brink: Experiences of the Void from a Depth Psychology Perspective (Karnac Books).

109. Stanley Greenspan & Stuart Shanker, 2004, The First Idea (Da Capo Press): 25.

110. Greenspan, First Idea: 37.

111. Greenspan, First Idea: 32.

112. Ken Robinson, 2009, The Element (Allen Lane): 8.

113. Vladimir Mayakovsky, 1930, from 'At the Top of My voice' (http://www.marxists.org/subject/art/literature/mayakovsky/1930/at-top-my-voice.htm).

114. Virginia Woolf, 1995, Killing the Angel in the House (Penguin 60s).

115. Ruth Padel, 2004, from 52 Ways of Looking at a Poem, published by Chatto & Windus: 18. Reprinted by permission of The Random House Group Limited.

116. Seni Seniviratne, Beyond Reconciliation Conference, UCT December 2009. Courtesy Seni Seniviratne.

117. A. H. Modell, 1997, 'Reflections on metaphors and affects,' Annual of Psychoanalysis, 25:219–33.

118. J. Gardner, 1993, Journal of Poetry Therapy, Vol. 6, (4):213–27.

119. I. Tegnér, 2009, Journal of Poetry Therapy, Vol. 22 (3):121–31.

120. W. B. Yeats, 1996, from 'Byzantium,' The Collected Poems of W. B. Yeats (Scribner): 248.

121. Ted Hughes, 1995, Winter Pollen (Faber & Faber): 25.

122. Robinson, The Element: 16.

123. Robert Bosnak, 2007, Embodiment (Sussex: Routledge): 41.

124. Bosnak, Embodiment: 41–45.

125. Jung, 1981, C. G. Jung, Collected Works Vol. 13 (Routledge & Kegan Paul): 50, para 75.

126. Mindell, Dreaming Body.

127. Hollis, Bad Things: 203.

128. Dawn Garisch, from 'Into the valley', Difficult Gifts: 30
129. Werner Herzog, http://en.wikiquote.org/wiki/Werner_Herzog.
130. Lena Vasileva, 2008, Psyche and the Arts (Routledge), Ch. 8.
131. Greenspan, First Idea: 4.
132. Pert, Molecules: 183.
133. Pert, Molecules: 173.
134. Pert, Molecules: 26.
135. Padel, 52 Ways: 25.
136. Hyde, Trickster: 59.
137. Garisch, Difficult Gifts: 34.
138. Mindell, Dreaming Body: 37.
139. D. H. Lawrence, from 'The Song Of A Man Who Has Come Through,' Poem for the Day: 205.
140. Milner, Experiment: ix.
141. Jung, from an interview in the Good Housekeeping magazine, Dec. 1961.
142. W. Szymborska, 1995, from 'Discovery', View with a Grain of Sand (Harcourt & Brace): 75.
143. Jung, C.W., Vol. 5:438, para. 680.
144. Puleng Nkomo, 2011, from 'In my neighbourhood', The Sol Plaatje EU Poetry Anthology (Jacana Media): 78. Courtesy the poet.
145. David Cronenberg, 1992, Cronenberg on Cronenberg (Faber & Faber).
146. Jung, 1981, C.W., Vol. 7:174, para. 267.
147. Geoffrey Haresnape, 2011, from 'my mentor is dressing me', in Where the Wind Wills (Echoing Green Press): 34. Courtesy the poet.
148. Mindell, Dreaming Body: 67–71.
149. Colleen Higgs, 2011, from 'the other side', Lava Lamp Poems (Cape Town: Modjaji Books): 12. Courtesy the poet.
150. Augusten Burroughs, 2006, Possible Side Effects (London: Atlantic Books): 120–121.
151. Hollis, Bad Things: 64.

152. A. N. Schore, 2001, The right brain as the neurological substratum of Freud's dynamic unconscious.

153. A. N. Schore, 2001, 'Minds in the making,' British Journal of Psychotherapy.

154. Lyn Cozolino, 2002, The Neuroscience of Psychotherapy (W. W. Norton & Company).

155. C. S. Lewis, 1980, Till We Shall Have Faces (Harvest Books): 253.

156. John Muir, 1911, My First Summer in the Sierra (Boston: Houghton Mifflin): 110.

157. Qiao Zhou, 'In vivo reprogramming of adult pancreatic exocrine cells to -cells' Nature 455:627–32.

158. http://www.nsf.gov/news/special_reports/science_nation/spidersilk.jsp.

159. Edward F. Edinger, 1994, The Anatomy of the Psyche: Alchemical Symbolism in Psychotherapy (Chicago: Open Court Publishing Company).

160. William Shakespeare, Hamlet, Act I sc. iii.

Acknowledgements

Many thanks to Colleen Higgs of Modjaji Books for her courage and commitment, to Ivan Vladislavic for an insightful structural edit, to Karen Jennings and Gill Gimberg for their sharp attention to detail, and to Natascha Mostert and Liné van Wyk for design.

The first manuscript contained a fair number of extracts from the work of famous poets resident in other countries, as well as a smattering of our own. When we began to apply for permission to use these extracts, we discovered that the costs involved were prohibitive. So I turned to other local poets to find equivalents to replace the famous. Of course, there was plenty of excellent material, and I am both proud and humbled to bring to your attention a small slice of the wealth of poetry we have in this country. What is more, their poems were offered in a spirit of collegiality. So, if you like these examples of their work, give yourself a treat and buy their collections.

I would also like to thank the publishers who gave permission for extracts to be printed in this book.

Both the Academic and Non-fiction Association of South Africa (ANFASA) and the National Arts Council (NAC) provided grants which enabled me to take time off to research and complete the book. Their help to writers is invaluable.

Many thanks to Jean Albert and her enthusiastic help in the C. G. Jung Centre library in Rosebank, Cape Town.

The following people read and commented on earlier drafts, and I am grateful for their assistance: Katherine Glenday, John Cartwright, David Hill, Ann Pargiter, Paul Ashton and Peter Lewis. To Katherine and Nicola Glenday, thank you for your creative integrity and your stunning cover. Thanks also to the many friends and strangers who said, 'I can't wait for the book to come out'.

After four years, here it is, at last.

Dawn Garisch

Other Modjaji Non-Fiction Titles

Undisciplined Heart
by **Jane Katjavivi**

Hemispheres
by **Karen Lazar**

Reclaiming the L-Word: Sapphos Daughters Out in Africa
edited by **Alleyn Diesel**

Hester se Brood
by **Hester van der Walt**

Invisible Earthquake: a woman's journal through stillbirth
by **Malika Ndlovu**

Swimming with Cobras
by **Rosemary Smith**

www.modjajibooks.co.za